The Evidence
for
VISIONS OF THE
VIRGIN MARY

An investigation of the evidence for Marian apparitions
and its implications.

Also in this series:

The Evidence
for
VISIONS OF THE
VIRGIN MARY

KEVIN McCLURE

Series Editor: Hilary Evans

THE AQUARIAN PRESS
Wellingborough, Northamptonshire

First published 1983
Fourth Impression 1985

British Library Cataloguing in Publication Data

McClure, Kevin
    The evidence for visions of the Virgin Mary.
    1. Mary, Virgin — Apparitions and miracles
    (Modern)
    I. Title
    231.7'3   BT650

ISBN 0-85030-351-6

*The Aquarian Press is part of the
Thorsons Publishing Group*

Printed and bound in Great Britain by
Whitstable Litho Ltd., Whitstable, Kent

CONTENTS

'THE EVIDENCE' Series is prepared by The Aquarian Press in collaboration with ASSAP (Association for the Scientific Study of Anomalous Phenomena) under the editorship of Hilary Evans. Each book in the series will give a comprehensive, impartial and up-to-date assessment of the evidence currently available for a particular phenomenon.

Each book is written by a recognized authority on the subject who is in a position both to give a comprehensive presentation of the facts and to analyse them in the light of his own experience and first-hand research.

—————————— ● ——————————

ASSAP (Association for the Scientific Study of Anomalous Phenomena) was founded in 1981 to bring together people working in different fields of anomaly research. It does not compete with other societies or organizations, but serves as a link organization enabling members of existing groups to share views and information and benefit from pooled resources. ASSAP issues its own publications, has its own research archives, library and other facilities, and holds periodic public conferences and training events in various parts of the country: ASSAP co-operates with local groups or, where none exists, may form one of its own.

ASSAP members include people from all walks of life who share a belief that it is the scientific approach which is most likely to solve these enigmas: they are neither uncritical 'believers' on the one hand, nor blinkered sceptics on the other, but are ready to go where the evidence leads them. If you sympathize with this attitude and would like to participate actively in our exciting pursuit of the truth, you may consider joining us. Write for fuller details to the Editor, Evidence Series, Aquarian Press, Denington Estate, Wellingborough NN8 2RQ.

ILLUSTRATIONS

*Note: Illustrations marked * have been supplied by the Mary Evans Picture Library.*

INTRODUCTION

This is not a religious book, nor an anti-religious one. At its simplest, it is an investigation into a remarkable and unusual area of-human experience; an in-depth report of what many adults and children have said has happened to them over the past thousand years or so. For that is about how long human beings – in Europe and the Americas – have been seeing and hearing visions of figures that have either identified themselves as the Virgin Mary, or have been interpreted in that way.

Yet it is not really as simple as that. Writing about visions and apparitions in general – about the paranormal, if you like – is relatively easy. People may report seeing fairies, or spacemen, or little devils with horns and tails, or abominable snowmen or whatever, and it is then just a matter of investigation, interviewing, and trying to find a reasonable explanation for what the person has seen. Though the witness may feel that he or she has a mission to fulfil – particularly in UFO cases – this is seldom a matter of importance to anyone else. You can quite reasonably treat each such experience in isolation, because it is very seldom that any two of these events appear to be directly and unarguably linked. But dealing with the vast numbers of reports and accounts of visions of the Virgin Mary in her various forms and aspects is an entirely different matter. If there is one argument I would usually readily accept as evidence for the validity and authenticity of a phenomenon, it is that it can be shown to have recurred, more or less independently, in a variety of times and places. And if there is one phenomenon that seems, on the surface at least, to provide such evidence, it is the visions of the Virgin Mary.

So that is the essence of this book: investigating, presenting, and assessing, as the title suggests, the evidence concerning the visions that have been occurring for so long, in so many different places. There are different factors that we can regard as being evidential in any specific case; and there are other factors that are evidential in support of the continuity between one case and another. In the first instance the strongest evidence, the ideal proof, would be a group of children, whom we knew had never heard of the historical figure of Mary, the Mother of Christ, reporting a detailed encounter in which the figure of a young woman of Jewish appearance spoke at length, identifying herself clearly, perhaps prophesying, perhaps healing. Sadly, the visions almost invariably occur in Roman Catholic countries, or contexts at least. There is no such case.

Instead, what we find is a clear line of development and interdependence among the visions and the visionaries. Some of the early visionaries seem naive, and their stories plain and simple. And some of the later child visionaries seem to know, already, what to do in the event of a Marian apparition, much as other children learn how to behave in a restaurant, or what to do when crossing the road. They experience what they interpret as one apparition, and suddenly begin to follow a complex pattern of behaviour copied from previous visionaries in previous years. We shall see many cases of this kind, and consequently it is often almost impossible to decide where a spontaneous event ends and a learned and conditioned response begins.

Bearing this in mind, I have tried in presenting the many case histories of visions in this book to stress certain points that can help us in assessing the authenticity of each vision itself, and the continuity between each and all of them. And where there is a series of visions experienced by one witness or group of witnesses (as is commonly the case) I have emphasized the early visions in the series, and drawn most of the evidence from them. This is on the assumption that the early visions are the more likely to have been unexpected and spontaneous, though this may not always be the case.

Because we are discussing the actions and attributes of one specific individual – though that individual is the Virgin Mary – I have tried to pick out aspects in which direct comparisons can be made, mostly concerning the actual appearance of the figure. Such aspects as complexion, build, colour and style of hair, clothing and ornamentation, nature of arrival and departure, and also the content of any communication with the witness, seem to be of particular importance. Wherever possible, these details are included in each case.

Of course, repetition and continuity between the visions is of much less significance if the witnesses in each case can be shown to have known anything about some of the previous visions. I have therefore recorded the salient facts about the background of each of the witnesses, and an outline of the extent of their general and religious education and knowledge. In this context, I have also tried to record where there was interaction between the witnesses and those with knowledge of other visions and of Catholic theology during the course of a vision or a series of visions. Such interaction is, as will become apparent, increasingly frequent as time goes on and we come to the more modern cases.

Certain aspects, some given pride of place in 'religious' accounts of the visions, I have regarded as being of less importance: in particular, the matter of the healings and conversions that are so often the natural, even inevitable consequence of a vision of the Virgin. In almost every major case after 1830, healing, pilgrimage and mass conversion go hand in hand. Frequently it is the 'miracle cures' that assure the lasting fame of a shrine or place of pilgrimage, rather than the visions themselves. I shall consider the matter of the cures when summing up the rest of the evidence; but it is worth pointing out at this stage that the healings seem to occur regardless of the authenticity of the vision to which they are apparently related: they occur even in the least convincing cases. My own opinion is that the healing is probably a separate, if equally fascinating, phenomenon, probably deriving from the *human* mind and body.

The greater part of this book is pure history, and is subject to the problems of conflicting testimony that face all historians. In several cases where there are accounts of the same event from different sources, these have often been inconsistent and contradictory in quite important respects. In some places in the text I have had the space to point out where these contradictions have arisen, but in most instances I have had to take the more difficult course and have tried, by balancing one version against another, to produce as authentic an account as possible of what actually happened. I have quoted eye-witness reports wherever possible, for what these may be worth, even though they were often composed years after the events. However, the overall method has prevented the giving of specific references in much of the book; for this I apologise, though the Bibliography does list most of the sources that I have had access to. This will make it a little difficult to check my accuracy, but it should allow the book to be used for the purpose I intended: to provide sufficiently objective accounts for the reader to make an independent decision as to what the visions may mean, and whence they may have come.

One problem seems to persist through all these accounts: what does the evidence, once established, actually prove? That the witnesses had visions that they believed to be of the Virgin Mary? Or that the witnesses had visions *of* the Virgin Mary? The answer to these two questions could suddenly push the material presented in this book out of the realms of simple history, and towards something of a greater significance altogether.

ONE:
THE EARLY VISIONS: 1061-1830

Like most of the stories from the same period, many of the early reports and accounts of visions and appearances of the Virgin Mary are clearly little more than legends. Even in certain cases from our own century there are, as we shall see, some surprisingly vague points, and inconsistencies that cannot be resolved. The situation is far worse for reports originally made before 1830, and the great majority of them are well beyond verification, or the uncovering, at this stage, of any further evidence.

However, the important point is that there *are* reports of visions from 900 years ago, though we can never be sure what form they actually took. And there have been cases of one kind and another reported ever since. On the basis that there is no smoke without fire, and that legends have to start somewhere, I am sure that we must take notice of at least the sheer quantity of this evidence. Because there *is* such a multitude of cases it is only possible to pick out a handful of the most typical, together with some of those that have proved to have had a lasting influence, or that seem to be part of a possible pattern of overall development in the history of Marian apparitions. There are very many others to be found.

To some extent, the visions seem to have come from nowhere: it appears to be impossible to trace what would be an ideal pattern, one in which the figure of the apparitional Virgin Mary has appeared regularly since the physical death of the physical Virgin Mary, a historical figure accepted as the Mother of Jesus by Christians and historians alike. On the contrary, much as the personality and cultus of Mary developed gradually through the troubled history of the Early Church, when most of the beliefs and tenets of Western Christianity were formulated by men who, though learned, seem often to have been less than holy, so too did the commonly-accepted image and idea of what a vision of the Virgin should involve. Of course, visionary experience of both secular and religious content has always been reported from all over the world. But in the case of Mary, it seems to have taken about a thousand years for a vision to win wide popular interest and credibility, and gain the credence lent by pilgrimage. Strangely enough, an English vision seems to have a claim at least equal to any other as the first of this kind.

Walsingham
The most important centre of pilgrimage on the British mainland is undoubtedly at Walsingham, in Norfolk. It has had a long and exciting history as a shrine, and many of the events since the original vision have been a source of mystery and wonder. I have spoken to many people, Catholics and non-Catholics, about their visits to Walsingham, and all have commented on the way in which they were moved by the place and its atmosphere. Yet I have been surprised by how little is known about the vision that led to the founding of the shrine at Walsingham, and by how vague many of the pilgrims are about the 'facts' as they have been handed down. It is as true in this case as it is in any other that, to a real believer, it is the current value of a shrine, or a method of devotion, that matters. Perhaps I am a little sceptical, and too analytical, but some of the story does seem a little odd.

It runs along these lines. In the year 1061 at Little Walsingham, a hamlet in Norfolk, one Richeldis, the lady of the manor, had three visions of the Virgin Mary. I cannot find a physical description, but the content of the communication is clear enough. Each vision was of Mary in the Nazareth home where Jesus had grown up, and Richeldis was told to build an exact copy of the house as seen in the visions on her own land at Walsingham. Though the first written account of the visions actually dates from as late as 1465, several accounts quote the Virgin's words, as follows: 'And there at Walsingham in this little house shall be held in remembrance the great joy of my salutation when St Gabriel told me I should through humility be the mother of God's Son.' She is said, too, to have issued specific dimensions for the construction of the house.

What follows is clearly legend, and no more than that; and it is moreover a story of which variants appear in other contexts, in other parts of the world. Richeldis instructed her craftsmen to build the house (in a completely eleventh-century Norfolk style, not that of Palestine 1000 years before) and they met great initial difficulties in commencing the job. They left the site for the night, only to return the next morning to find that the building had not only moved some seventy yards, but that it had also been completed by expert builders to a a very high standard, still in an entirely English style.

Thus, strangely, came about the first European Marian shrine. Nothing is said about the Virgin herself, which is unfortunate, but the wishes expressed are clear forerunners of the requests for chapels in many of the later visions. Why She should have chosen such an obscure method of obtaining the building of a centre of worship is not explained in any document that I have seen. But then, with the first written record dating from 305 years after the event, much of the original sense and reason of the incidents may have been lost.

Early European visions

Europe is traditionally the focus of the visions of the Virgin, and there are many accounts dating from the Middle Ages. They are seldom more than hearsay, and again beyond investigation, but they play an important part in the development of the later visions in Europe. Particularly, several of them seem to form a link between earlier pagan beliefs and experiences and those of an encroaching Roman Catholic Church. In these, Mary is more like a goddess figure, working miracles of conflict, intervention, and healing, than the Mother of God as we now understand her. The following are two typically anecdotal accounts taken from a delightful old collection entitled *Miracles of the Blessed Virgin Mary*, written around 1435-1440 by Johannes Herolt, and translated from the Latin by C. C. Swinton Bland.

In a certain convent once happened a very pleasing thing. There was a sister of approved life, very zealous in her worship of the Blessed Virgin Mary. Having once injured her knee by bending it too often in her devotions, at midday as she slept in the infirmary, she thought she saw the Blessed Virgin Mary stand by her in a dream carrying in her hand a box of ointment; who, putting her fingers into this, anointed the hurts of the nun with the ointment. And immediately there was such a sweet smell that the sister sleeping in the next room awakened by its fragrance rose and came to her bed, because the scent seemed to be stronger there, and roused the sleeper.

And when they asked whence the odour came she, although not ignorant of the cause, was unwilling to say anything to them and therefore would not tell them, so that they might go to sleep. And when they were again asleep, again the Mother of the Lord was present, leading her in a vision into the open space within the walls, and placing her hand under her chin she said 'Kneel down'. And when she had done this, our Lady added, 'In future you must thus ask humbly for pardon'.

In a church where it was the rule that the responsory 'Rejoice Mary' with the verse 'Gabriel' in which there is 'Let the Jew take shame', should be sung daily, a certain scholar, because of the sweetness of his voice, was ordered to sing it. Now some Jews passing in front of the church to their vineyards and, unable to endure the shame of the words, cautiously took the scholar and killed him in the vineyards. Soon afterwards, as they were leaving the vineyards, the Glorious Virgin Mary brought the boy back to life and commanded him to sing her praise with confidence. The Jews, again recognizing the voice and stricken with wonder, secretly questioned the boy. He replied that he had indeed been killed, but had been restored to his former life by his Queen. When the Jews knew this, no small number of them were converted to the glory of the Glorious Virgin Mary.[1]

You could almost replace the title 'Virgin Mary' in these accounts with that of any pagan goddess, and hardly notice the difference. But they make clear an aspect of the development of the character of the Virgin that comes increasingly to the fore: the Virgin as independent miracle-worker. Another aspect, an early form of the sort of sacrifice and self-denial later called for at Fatima, appears in a Spanish account first published around 1410:

Saint Gregory in the *Dialogues* tells of a girl to whom the Virgin Mary appeared, showed some other girls of her age, and asked if she wanted to be with them. She replied that she would. And the Virgin Mary said to her, 'Then from now on do nothing that the other girls do', and also told her to keep away from foolishness and games, and that in thirty days she would come to be with the virgins she had seen. The girl did this, and when she was dying after thirty days she saw the Virgin with the girls she had come with the first time, and the Virgin called her. She replied twice, 'Lady I come, Lady I come'. And saying this she gave up her soul to God, and thus died in the company of the holy virgins. From which it clearly appears that it is forbidden to holy virgins to be at dances.[2]

Such accounts are numerous, as are others in which the Virgin seems to take a close interest in local social or religious politics. These cases seem to be so far from spontaneous that they have little value for us as evidence; they seem to be the product of folklore at best, of sheer fabrication at worst. We have presented sufficient legends: it is time we moved on to more evidential material.

Our Lady of Guadalupe

Walsingham aside, there is little verification available for
the cases we have mentioned so far: what you have read of

N. S. DE MISERICORDIA, CON SUS TRES, MARTI.S
VENERADOS EN SU ERMITA DE LA VILLA DE REUS.

Artist's representation of an early Spanish apparition at Reus.

each case is all that there is. Yet suddenly, we have a much reported case, the subject of several excellent books, as early as 1531, and in Mexico of all places. It has to be said that the first written report presenting the story of the vision itself was made in 1560, twenty-nine years later, so whatever was written subsequently has to be built on rather shaky foundations.

All the accounts I have seen of Guadalupe display elements of romanticizing, but there is a general consensus, which I will retell briefly here. Early in the morning of 9 December 1531, five miles north of Mexico City, a 57-year-old Aztec Indian by the name of Juan Diego was running to attend mass in the nearest village with a church. As he reached the foot of a hill known as Tepeyac, where there had been in the past a temple to the Aztec Mother Goddess (a point worth noting), there seemed to be a sudden silence, broken by a woman's voice calling his name. The sun had barely risen, but Juan saw, surrounded by golden beams of light, a young Mexican girl of about fourteen years. She was said to be beautiful, but I have not found any reliable description of her.

She told Juan that she required a chapel to be built at the site of the vision, and then instructed him to run to the Bishop at Mexico City and pass on the message. This Juan did and, after some delay, obtained an audience. The Bishop, it seems, was not unreasonable, and said that Juan could visit him again, though he promised nothing. Juan went away home, and on the journey again saw the figure he took to be the Virgin Mary, at the same spot. She comforted him, and told him to try again at Mexico City the next day, Sunday.

The next morning, having been to mass, Juan returned to Bishop Zumarraga. Again, he was tolerant if uncertain, and finally he asked Juan if his vision could produce some sort of sign, by way of proof. On his way back home to visit Juan Bernardino, an uncle of his who was seriously ill, he saw the vision once more, and she promised that she would provide a sign the following morning. When Juan returned the next morning he was expecting his

uncle to die and told the figure about his fears. She at
once assured him that Juan Bernardino's health was
restored at that instant, and went on to tell him to pick
some flowers from the top of the hill, though the season
should have precluded their growth. Flowers there were,
however, which may well have been Castilian roses.
Juan picked a few, and took them to the Bishop folded-up
in his long outer cape, known as a *tilma*.

Then, in a fashion that features in a number of other
legends, such as the Veil of St Veronica, a miracle was

Our Lady of Guadalupe: the miraculous image.

seen to have occurred. As Juan unfolded the *tilma* it emerged that the image of the girl he had seen and spoken to was imprinted on it, in full colour. The Bishop and others fell to their knees, and it was commanded that the cloth should be taken and hung up on the wall of the Bishop's private chapel. Furthermore, when Juan went back to his uncle, he found the old man fully recovered, and telling of how he had been healed by a glowing young woman who had said to him: 'Call me and my image Santa Maria de Guadalupe'.

However the image may have originated, it is still on display in Mexico and is surrounded by all the trappings of a centre of massive pilgrimage. Some wild claims are made for the content of the image, and Francis Johnston[3] suggests that in the eyes of the image can be seen representations of the witnesses who were present in the Bishop's room when, supposedly, the miracle took place – because these very people would have been reflected in the eyes of the Virgin herself at the time. Sadly, the evidence presented for this claim is very hard to accept. Overall, the effects of Guadalupe are better catalogued by far than are its origins. It is difficult to know what is of value as evidence here, and what is not.

Le Laus

A case that is rarely mentioned seems to provide a tenuous link between the early cases and those of the nineteenth and twentieth centuries, in that it anticipates some of the features characteristic of the visions to children. This apparition occurred in the Grenoble area of the French Alps, and the sole witness was one Benoit Rencurel, a devout shepherdess of seventeen. In May 1664 she was out working on a hillside near a ruined chapel and had just finished saying her rosary when an elderly man in a red robe appeared to her, introducing himself as St Maurice. He found for her a spring of water that she had not seen before, and then told her to go with her sheep to a small valley near St Etienne, 'where a great grace would be granted her'.

Being a devout girl, she went to the valley the next day. At a spot known as Les Fours she saw the first of a series of visions of a lady and child that were to occur regularly over a period of two months. Eventually, on the advice of a local magistrate, Benoit asked the figure who she was (it is, perhaps, surprising that she had not done so before). The figure is said to have replied: 'I am Mary, the Mother of Jesus. It is the will of my son that I should be honoured in this parish, though not in this spot. You will therefore ask the priest to come here with his people in procession.'

The local priest complied with this request, on 29 August 1664. There were no further events till 29 September when, on the road to Le Laus, the lady again appeared. 'Go to Le Laus,' she said. 'There you will find a little chapel where delicious perfumes abound. There you will often find and see me.' Benoit did as she was told, and at Le Laus found a ruined chapel, which the lady, appearing again, told her would be enshrined in a large church. She went on: 'I have requested Le Laus from my divine son for the conversion of sinners and He has given it to me. The church will be built in his honour and mine. Many sinners will be converted here.'

Much of this actually happened, despite persistent problems in Church politics in the diocese, and Pope Leo XIII declared the church, when built, to be a Roman basilica, conferring considerable status on it. A number of healings and miraculous cures were claimed, and accepted by ecclesiastical authorities. In 1871 (the year of the vision at Pontmain) Benoit Rencurel was declared Venerable by Pope Pius IX. Le Laus may be an evidential case for its age.

Catherine Labouré and the Miraculous Medal
Though the period from 1700 to 1820 saw many dramatic changes in the face of conventional religious movements, and though it saw a great number of developments in the social and industrial life of much of Europe, it is also a period almost devoid of significant claims of visions of the Virgin. There is no apparent reason for this, and we

have to move on to Paris in 1830 for the next vision of importance.

The reports concerning Catherine Labouré and the inception of the devotional object known as the Miraculous Medal are famous and, it appears, relatively well-researched. Insofar as they were experienced by, and only by, an extremely devout 'religious', a member of a holy order, who seems to have keenly anticipated just such an event, I do not feel that these reports have the same evidential value as the later, more probably 'spontaneous', visions witnessed by children. However, the popularity of the Medal itself, and of the images it bore, may well prove to be a factor in the content of later visions, and in the assessment of *their* value as evidence.

Catherine Labouré was born with the given name of Zoe to a farming family in the Côte d'Or in the year 1806. Her mother died when she was eight, and the young child took over much of her work; she also kept seven or eight hundred pigeons (I have failed to find out why!). She was clearly a devout Catholic child, who later made claim to extensive early religious experience, and in 1830 at the age of twenty-four she entered the convent of the Sisters of Charity in the Rue de Bac in Paris.

Within a few days of her arrival there, she told her colleagues that she had seen a vision of the heart of St Vincent, glowing above a case containing some of his relics. No secret is made in the accounts of her life that it was her dearest ambition to see the Virgin Mary, and that she frequently prayed to both her guardian angel and to St Vincent that this favour should be granted to her. The Catholic Truth Society booklet on the subject goes so far as to say that: On the 18th of July, the eve of St Vincent's feast, she went to bed convinced that her holy patron would obtain her wish.'

The story of that night is this. At about 11.30 pm the visionary heard her name called three times and woke up to see a child of four or five with golden hair, glowing with light. (This was, presumably, her guardian angel.) The child told her to go to the convent chapel, which she found to be brightly illuminated. Just on midnight, the Virgin Mary appeared, clad in a white robe and blue veil, and sat in the chair of the Director of the religious house. The figure told Catherine that she had a mission to perform that would cause her suffering, and then made, apparently, a number of prophecies. These included the future death by violence of the Archbishop of Paris and have been interpreted, with some plausibility, as referring to events in the Paris Commune in 1870 to 1871.

Catherine Labouré saw no more visions till 27 November, when she was praying in the chapel at about 5.30 pm. The Virgin appeared dressed all in white, with a floor-length white veil. She stood upon a half-globe, round which was twined a green serpent with yellow spots. She held a golden globe surmounted by a cross, which she explained represented the world. She wore three rings on each finger, and each ring emitted brilliant rays of light.

The photographic quality of the vision now becomes apparent. As Labouré later described it,

A frame, slightly oval in shape, formed round the Blessed Virgin. Within it was written in letters of gold, 'O Mary, conceived without sin, pray for us who have recourse to thee'.

The inscription, in a semi-circle, began at the height of the right hand, passed over the head, and finished at the left hand. The golden ball disappeared in the brilliance of the sheaves of light bursting from all sides; the hands turned out, and the arms were bent down under the weight of the treasures of grace obtained. Then the voice said,

'Have a medal struck after this model. All who wear it will receive great graces; they should wear it around the neck. Graces will abound for those who wear it with confidence.'

At this instant the tableau seemed to me to turn, and I beheld the reverse of the medal: a large 'M' surmounted by a bar and a cross; beneath the 'M' were the hearts of Jesus and Mary, the one crowned with thorns, the other pierced with a sword.

The visionary later said that the figure then disappeared 'like a candle blown out'.

The remainder of the life of Catherine Labouré was spent in a subtle campaign (not easy to conduct from within the walls of a convent) to have the Medal manufactured and distributed, while still trying not to disclose her identity, which she contrived to do till 1876, only six months before her death. The Medal was first struck, or pressed, in 1832, and it quickly became known as the 'Miraculous Medal'. Millions have been distributed, and countless cures and conversions have been attributed to its power. In 1895 it was accorded a Mass and office of its own within the Roman Catholic liturgy, and as such it has

HAVE A MEDAL STRUCK.
GRACES WILL ABOUND FOR THOSE
WHO WEAR IT WITH CONFIDENCE

Postcard celebrating the centenary of the Miraculous Medal.

an almost unique position. It is beyond doubt that its popularity in the years immediately following 1832 played a considerable part in the declaration of the doctrine of the Immaculate Conception in 1854; a doctrine that was in turn to play an important part in the acceptance of the Lourdes visions as authentic in 1858.

An unavoidable consequence of the widespread popularity of the Medal developing so soon after the vision that inspired it is that we must approach the claims of any French visionary in the following years with some caution; there are in fact several of them. An image on a devotional object is easy to remember, and could make a lasting impression on a child, even a very young one. The memory might not be a conscious one, and might not be recalled when the visionary is interviewed and, as most were, interrogated. It seems highly likely that, as we shall find, Bernadette Soubirous of Lourdes knew the Medal well, and probably the children at Pontmain too, where the image of the vision bears some striking similarities to the Medal. Aside from its own story and significance, the Miraculous Medal may well have had a powerful influence on other reports of visions of the Virgin that we shall be considering, in two possible ways. Now that such marvellous events had happened to one ordinary, if devout, young girl, why shouldn't they happen to another? And now that an image, a pattern, had been established for what a vision could like like, how much more common might such visions become?

TWO:
'If we had known it was a great saint, we would have asked her to take us with her'

LA SALETTE, FRANCE, 19 SEPTEMBER 1846

Suddenly, almost literally out of the blue, from the sky over Ablandins near Grenoble in France in 1846, came a new kind of vision of the Virgin Mary, one that was to set a pattern that still persists. Before then, the great majority of visions had been experienced by those with a clear predisposition to receiving them, by virtue of their devout lives, which had often led them to the shelter of a religious order.

Of course there had been exceptions, and visions of other kinds – from fairies to demons – had been seen by many different types of people. But there had been no hint that the developments observable at La Salette were on their way. For here the witnesses involved were children, and children from a less than keenly religious background. The vision that they had, and the prophecies given during it, still echo in the most modern of visionary experiences.

There were two witnesses, a girl and a boy. It is well worth looking closely at their personal and social background, for if there is a conventional explanation to be found, such factors are bound to play an important part in it.

Melanie Mathieu was born on 7 November 1831. Even by the standards of rural France in those difficult, unsettled years, she had lived a wretched life. One of eight children, her father worked in a timber yard and never earned sufficient money to adequately support them all. At an age when our children are just settling down at their first school, she was out begging in the streets of Corps, the small town in which she lived. When she was eight she started working, at least nine months a year, as a herder and shepherdess for various of the small farmers in the hamlets that made up the commune of La Salette. She only returned to live with her parents in Corps for the hardest of the winter months; December, January and February each year were spent caring for her brothers and sisters. She was not known as a bright girl, and it has been said that she would on occasion sleep outside in the rain because she did not think to take shelter in the stable with the animals. We are hardly in a position to criticize her standard of education; she had no chance of any. But even after the vision, when the nuns tried to teach her the Catechism, the found it a painfully unrewarding task.

Maximin Giraud was born on 27 August 1835. His mother died soon after he was born, and though his father was a wheelwright – a sound enough trade in the main road town of Corps – he lived in considerable poverty. His father drank too much and spent little time at the family home. Maximin often passed most of his day hanging around the cafes where his father did his drinking. Perhaps his life was not quite as arduous as Melanie's seems to have been – collecting horse droppings was his only positive contribution to the family budget – and he spent most of his time playing with his dog, Loulou, the third witness of the vision. He was similarly devoid of any formal education, and of any sophisticated degree of religious knowledge.

It is claimed, in favour of the truth and spontaneity of the vision, that Maximin (known as Memin) and Melanie had never met till shortly before it occurred. However, that they lived at opposite ends of a town of only about 1000 people is a strong argument against that contention. Also, Maximin was clearly well-acquainted with Melanie's employer at the time of the vision, and it was to him that

Maximin gave his first account of what had happened. I am not sure how important these facts may be, but we should note any less than factual element in the story as it has been passed down.

Certainly, it seems to have been chance that threw the children together in the week of the vision. Melanie was, at fourteen, a skilled herder who would not have difficulty finding work, though she could expect little payment for it over and above her keep. Maximin knew no trade, and only because the herder employed by an Ablandins farmer, Pierre Selme, had fallen ill, did Selme come to Corps to ask Maximin's father if he could stand in for a week. Giraud senior asked a high price for his son's services, and insisted that Selme should keep a watch on the boy on the dangerous hillsides where the cattle were grazed. Selme agreed because he needed the help and so, on Thursday 17 September 1846, Melanie and Maximin found themselves on the same hillside, supposedly meeting for the first time.

There is no reason to suspect that these two had much in common, or that they had any motivation for colluding in inventing the story of the vision. One was a feckless eleven-year-old in his first week of work, playing with his dog. The other was a dour, quiet fourteen-year-old, hard-working, following her trade. But they were on adjoining strips of land on a rocky hillside 6000 feet above sea level, and there is no doubt that they were familiar at least to each other prior to the event that was to change their lives and, indirectly, a great many others.

On the morning of the Saturday of the great event there is some reason to believe the children had been playing a sort of religious game involving the building of a miniature altar known as a 'paradis'. This argues somewhat against the usual version, in which the children are said to have had no conscious interest in, or knowledge of, religious matters, and it is seldom mentioned in accounts of La Salette for fear of detracting from the children's apparent innocence and naivety. Howsoever, at about three o'clock in the afternoon, the children

Véritables Portraits.

MAXIMIN.   MÉLANIE.

The witnesses at La Salette: a contemporary engraving.

awoke after sleeping on the ground for an hour or more. They had eaten earlier, just rye bread dipped in the water of a nearby stream. Of course, there is a tendency towards misperception immediately after waking.

Despite his assurance that he would keep an eye on the boy, Pierre Selme seems to have been out of sight of the children at this time. Melanie first saw the beginning of the vision as she turned round to look for the bags in which they had brought their food. Only the children actually witnessed the vision, and heard what was said.

At this point, I think that it is important that we go back to the earliest account available of the vision in English. Indeed, it is the earliest account I have found in any language. This is in *The Holy Mountain of La Salette* by the Most Reverend William Ullathorne.[4] Ullathorne was Archbishop of Birmingham and made an extensive trip to La Salette a few years after the events there. During this trip he saw the witnesses, and interviewed those to whom they had first told their stories and the civil and ecclesiastical authorities involved in the earliest assessments of their veracity. He first published his account of his expedition in 1854, and as one of the remarkable features of this case is the almost perfect consistency in the witnesses' description of the vision throughout their lives, Ullathorne's version of Melanie's account of the events of that afternoon is probably as close to real evidence as we can come, 140 years later.

Melanie's Recital

We fell asleep . . . then I woke first, and I did not see my cows. I woke Maximin. 'Maximin,' I said, 'quick, let us go and look for the cows.' We passed the little stream which went up straight before us, and saw the cows lying down on the other side; they were not far off. I was coming down first, and when I was five or six steps off the little stream, I saw a brightness like the sun, it was far more brilliant, but it had not the same colour. And I said to Maximin, 'Come, quick, and see the bright light down there'; and Maximin came down saying, 'Where is it?' I pointed to it near the little spring, and he stopped when he saw it. Then we saw a lady in the bright light; she was sitting with her head in her hands. We were afraid; I let my stick fall. Then Maximin said, 'Keep your stick; if it does anything I will give it a good knock.' Then the lady rose up, crossed her arms, and said to us, 'Come near, my children, be not afraid. I am here to tell you great news.' Then we crossed the little stream, and she advanced to the place where we had been sleeping. She was between us both. She said to us weeping all the time that she spoke (I clearly saw her tears falling):

'If my people will not submit, I shall be forced to let go the hand of my son. It is so strong, so heavy, that I can no longer withhold it.

'For how long a time do I suffer for you! If I would not have my Son abandon you, I am compelled to pray to Him without ceasing. And as to you, you take no heed of it.

'However much you pray, however much you do, you will never recompense the pains I have taken for you.

'Six days have I given you to labour, the seventh I have kept for myself, and they will not give it to me. It is this which makes the hand of my Son so heavy. Those who drive the carts cannot swear without introducing the name of my Son. These are the two things which make the hand of my Son so heavy. If the harvest is spoilt, it is all on your account. I gave you warning last year in the potatoes but you did not heed it. On the contrary, when you found the potatoes spoilt, you swore, you took the name of my Son in vain. They will continue to decay, so that by Christmas there will be none left.'

I must intrude here to point out that the two children did not normally speak French, and had only a limited knowledge of it. They usually spoke in *patois*, the language of their district. At the talk of potatoes Melanie, who up till now had more or less understood what the lady had said in French, began to flounder, and the lady apparently realized this. The remainder of the message was given in *patois*.

'Ah, my Children, you do not understand; I will say it in a different way.' Then she continued.

'If you have wheat it is no good to sow it; all that you sow the insects will eat. What comes up will fall into dust when you thrash it.

'There will come a great famine. Before the famine comes, the children under seven years of age will be seized with trembling, and will die in the hands of those that hold them; and others will do penance by the famine.

'The walnuts will become bad, the grapes will rot. If they are converted, the stones and the rocks will change into loads of wheat, and the potatoes will be self-sown on the lands.

'Do you say your prayers well, my children?' Both of us answered, 'Not very well, madam.'

'You must be sure to say them well, morning and evening. When you cannot do better, say at least an 'Our Father' and a 'Hail Mary'. But when you have time, say more.

'There are none who go to mass but a few aged women, the rest work on a Sunday all the summer; and in the winter, when they know not what to do, they go to mass, only to mock at religion. During Lent, they go to the shambles like dogs . . .'

After this the lady told us,

'Well, my children, you will make this known to all my people.'

Then she ascended to the place where we had gone to look for our cows. She did not touch the grass. She moved along on the tips of the grass. I and Maximin followed her. I passed before the lady, and Maximin a little on the side, two or three steps. And then the beautiful lady arose a little from the ground, then she looked towards heaven, then towards the earth; then we saw her head no more, then her arms no more, then her feet no more; we saw nothing more but a brightness in the air; after this the brightness disappeared. And I said to Maximin,

'Perhaps it is a great saint,' and Maximin said to me,

'If we had known it was a great saint, we would have asked her to take us with her.'

And I said to him, 'O that she were here still.'

Then Maximin darted his hand out to catch a little of the brightness; but there was nothing there any more. And we looked well, to see if we could not see her. And I said, 'She will not let herself be seen, that we may not see where she goes.' Afterwards we looked after our cows.

When asked about the lady's appearance (and it should be stressed that both children always referred to her as

'The Lady' rather than giving her any kind of religious title), she replied:

She had white shoes, with roses round them of all colours, a gold-coloured apron, a white robe with pearls all over it, a white cape over her shoulders with roses round it; a white cap, bent a little forwards; a crown with roses round her cap. She wore a very small chain, on which was hung a cross with a figure of our Lord; on the right were pincers, on the left a hammer. At the extremities of the cross another large chain fell, like the roses round the cape. Her face was white and elongated. I could not look at her long together, because she dazzled us.

Maximin agreed entirely with this description when he gave his version of events, and on the whole the remainder of his account replicated Melanie's. It is interesting, however, to note that he says,

Then, as we were coming down, Melanie saw a great brightness on towards the spring, and she said to me,
    'Maximin, come and see this brightness.' I went towards Melanie, *then we saw the brightness open* and within it we saw a lady sitting like this.

Does this statement somehow prefigure later appearances of figures and entities from other balls of light – such as UFOs?

It also appears that a 'secret' was imparted to each of the children, neither hearing what was said to the other during this part of the message. As children, neither of the witnesses would reveal these secrets, though Melanie apparently did so much later in life. If that version is to be taken seriously, its content was much the sort of prediction of tribulation and suffering if the world does not turn to the Church as we will later find conveyed at Fatima and Garabandal.

The matter of the later lives of the witnesses has been used to cast doubt upon the authenticity of the vision itself. Maximin drifted with little direction or success from one job to another, while Melanie, who seemed to wish to live the life of a nun, tried unsuccessfully to fit into a number of religious orders, including several years at a Carmelite convent in Darlington, England. As time went on she started calling herself, 'Sister Mary of the Cross, Victim of Jesus', and it does seem that she became rather opinionated, difficult to get on with, and perhaps somewhat eccentric. It is certainly true that their experience brought little happiness to either of them in later life, but neither of them ever wavered from their version of the events of 19 September, and both retained a deep devotion to their faith till the last. It would be wrong to judge the vision in the light of their later shortcomings.

The final point it is vital to consider is that of the prophecies, which are exceptionally specific. It does appear that the majority of them were fulfilled within a short space of time. By the end of 1846 potatoes could not be bought in the area. *Phylloxera* struck the grape crop. A form of cholera affecting only young children, and causing two hours of shaking and sickness before almost certain death, reached epidemic proportions. The walnut crop failed. Even the most cynical of commentators concur with these points.

We shall consider the matter of the prophecies again, and of the healings that resulted from the application of water from a stream rising from a spring that started flowing out of season after the vision, when we come to our conclusions. For now, there seems to be evidence enough to suggest that the claims of the visionaries at La Salette should be taken very seriously indeed.

THREE:
'I don't promise to make you happy in this world, but in the next'
LOURDES, FRANCE, FEBRUARY TO JULY 1858

Lourdes is the most famous of the Marian apparitions, and writing about it presents a number of problems. In several of the cases dealt with in this book I have been disappointed by the small amount of source material available for use in research, but with Lourdes the problem is entirely different. There are so many books (well over a hundred in one library I have been using) that deal with one aspect or another of Lourdes that it is hard to know where to begin. From Emile Zola's cynical and dismissive novel *Lourdes* (1894), which finds only deceit and dishonour where there was probably little or none, to the sycophantic and oft-repeated film *The Song of Bernadette*, all that the world at large has been fed with for many years is interpretation. It is not easy to dig out the original facts – and in some instances where I seem to have done so, the results have been less than impressive.

What has made Lourdes famous – and Bernadette the only Saint among the child visionaries – is the healing 'miracles' that have taken place at and because of the shrine there. I would not argue with many of the claims for healing – or, to put it more accurately, for people getting better because of their contact with Lourdes – and we can look at these together with the many other similar claims in our conclusions. But our brief is the visions, and it is the visions that I have attempted to investigate. Faced with such a multitude of sources, often different from each other on minor, but significant, points, I have done my best to weigh what appears to be the important evidence, and have taken it from the most apparently reliable sources wherever they concur – though this does not of course guarantee veracity.

It is necessary, in this much-publicized case more than any other, to look closely at the personal and social background of the one witness, for it seems to have played a major part in what took place. If the children at La Salette came from a background of poverty and hardship, then Bernadette certainly saw even worse. She was born on 7 January 1844 at Boly Mill in the castle town of Lourdes. Her father, Francois Soubirous, was a miller with a reputation for inefficiency, and when his mother moved out of the mill the business went into a gradual decline. When Bernadette was eight he was remilling the millstones when a chip of stone flew out and blinded his left eye. Such was his luck. Meanwhile his wife, Louise, fared little better, suffering from severe burns when the child was eleven months old, so that Bernadette had to be sent off to a wet nurse. This was at the nearby village of Bartres, and the child did not return to Boly until April 1846.

Francois had never actually earned enough to buy the mill, the occupation of which he had inherited from his father, and following his injury the situation became so untenable that the family had to leave Boly. They moved about, living in a variety of rented accommodation, and Soubirous took such labouring jobs as were available to him. In the autumn of 1855 a cholera epidemic attacked Lourdes, and Bernadette, never a strong child, caught it. She survived while many did not, but the sickness had its effect, and from then on she was never free of bronchial asthma. Nor was cholera the only disaster to befall the people of Lourdes: a famine, already threatening, became worse because the harvest could not be properly carried out. Hunger led to civil unrest, which was put down by military force. At this time Bernadette was loaned out to her Aunt Bernarde, where she earned her keep by working in her aunt's bar, and by looking after her aunt's children. Not much of a life for a child of eleven.

By the time Bernadette returned to her family, the situation was worse than ever. It is part of the romance of Lourdes to contrast the sanctity of the child with the squalor of her surroundings, but there is considerable truth in it. It is probably true that the only furniture they had to take from one squalid lodging to another was two beds and a storage box, the rest having been sold. There is no doubt that the family, having proved themselves hopeless tenants, were at the time of the first vision living in the only free accommodation that they could find: one room in the old prison building, a building that had fallen into disuse because it was regarded as unfit for the convicts! The room had two windows, without glass. Both looked out on a dung heap, and the open prison lavatory system.

The spring of 1857 saw even worse disgrace for the family, when Francois Soubirous was arrested and imprisoned for theft. He was released for lack of evidence, but the trouble made finding work even harder. Both parents drank to such excess as they could afford, to the detriment of the four children. Again it seems to be true, that the five-year-old boy was found in such a state of hunger that he was eating candle-wax from the church floor.

Later the same year, for sound economic reasons, Bernadette was sent off again, this time to join Marie Lagues at Bartres, who had wet-nursed her as a child. She stayed there for between four and seven months (despite her later fame, many aspects of Bernadette's early life are surprisingly uncertain), and only returned to her family in January 1858. In the influence that these few months had on Bernadette, in particular on her religious knowledge and attitudes, may well lie the key to the meaning of the Lourdes visions, and to the assessment of the evidence in this case. Her parents had made it a condition of her departure that she should be taught the catechism while she was away – and a fiery manner it was taught in, too – so that she could take her first communion. But the Lagues home was more than usually religious, for Lagues' brother was a priest, and a very frequent visitor. It is necessary, when considering the evidence presented by the appearance and pronouncements of the visions in 1858, to consider what Bernadette might, consciously or otherwise, have taken in during these months away from home.

Through her acquaintance with these religious people, over a sustained period, Bernadette may well have learned a good deal about both previous visions to girls not unlike herself – Catherine Labouré and Melanie Calvat, for instance – and also about events and pronouncements within the Roman Catholic Church itself. Surely it would have been natural for a priest to come home and tell his sister about his business: even if that business was the priesthood. Much has been made of the announcement of her vision to Bernadette, 'I am the Immaculate Conception'. It is widely supposed that this was a unique and independent confirmation of what had been proclaimed as doctrine by the Pope four years previously. But it must at least be possible that Bernadette heard of it first at the dining table at Bartres, rather than in the Grotto at Lourdes. We should certainly bear this in mind as we consider the visions themselves.

The life at Bartres seems to have been too harsh for the child, for she returned by choice to the little prison room. Having no proper employment she spent her time minding the children, or earning a little from odd jobs. One of these was collecting bones, which could then be sold. In Lourdes such scavenging was best done by the Massabielle cliff, where the bones of drowned animals were caught as they swept downstream. For this reason, and also because there was firewood nearby, Bernadette, Toinette her younger sister, and a friend, Jeanne Abadie, found themselves at Massabielle at about midday on 11 February 1858.

The three children decided to cross the stream at the base of the cliff. Toinette and Jeanne waded across – the asthmatic Bernadette was more cautious. It is unfortunate, and not a little surprising, that the first eye-witness report of this incident that has any authority appears to date from as late as 28 May 1861, but it must be quoted, and assumed to be important evidence:

I went a bit further to see if I could cross without taking off my shoes and stockings, I could not. Then I went back in front of the grotto to take off my shoes and stockings. As I began I heard a noise. I turned towards the meadow and I saw the trees were not moving at all. I went on taking off my shoes and stockings. I heard the same noise. I raised my head and looked at the grotto. I saw a lady dressed in white, she was wearing a white dress and a blue sash and a yellow rose on each foot the colour of the chain of her rosary. When I saw that I rubbed my eyes – I thought I was seeing things. I put my hand in my pocket and I found my rosary in it. I wanted to make the sign of the cross but I could not get my hand up to my forehead, it fell back. The vision made the sign of the cross, then my hand shook. I tried to make it and I could, I said my rosary. The vision ran the beads of hers through her fingers but she did not move her lips. When I had finished my rosary, the vision disappeared all of a sudden...

As this account was recorded more than three years after the event, it is worth comparing it with snippets that have survived from earlier events. The important thing is that there is already a romantic vision of Lourdes developing. It seems that when Bernadette went to confession two days after the first vision all that she told the priest was that she had seen something white in the shape of a woman or a girl; certainly, the name she gave to the vision till later in the series of apparitions was *Aquero*, which translated from the local Bigourdan dialect means, more or less, 'that one' or 'that thing'. Also, the child initially described the vision as being about her own age: fourteen. And Bernadette herself was small for her age. The 1861 description makes the figure seem peculiarly like a representation of the Miraculous Medal, and also like the statuary that even then was becoming common in the

The Grotto at Lourdes at the time of the first vision in 1858.

town. It is noticeable that statues of Our Lady of Lourdes seldom, if ever, represent a small teenage girl in white. But that is probably the fault of history and commerce; it does not necessarily detract from the authenticity of the visions themselves.

It seems likely that Bernadette entered a state of ecstasy – lost in her own emotions, oblivious to most physical sensation – on this first occasion. When she crossed the millstream she did not feel the bitter cold. She went into a similar state during the second apparition, on the Sunday, 14 February, when she went to the grotto 'as if impelled to do so', followed by ten or twelve other young girls. Except that Bernadette had come equipped with holy water, which she cast at the vision in case it derived from the Devil, and which she sprinkled to no apparent effect, much the same happened as on the Thursday. However, Bernadette had to be helped home by two adults.

The theory now went the rounds that the apparition was of one Elisa Latapie, a devout Catholic girl who had died on 2 October 1857, at the age of twenty-eight.

Consequently, when Bernadette went to the grotto on Thursday, 18 February, she was accompanied by two local women, one a relative of the 'ghost', and was armed with pen and paper. These precautions say much about how uncertain was the identification of the figure at this stage.

This time, urged on by the adults, Bernadette took the

Bernadette Soubirous: a photograph taken in the year of the visions.

initiative instead of merely kneeling and saying her rosary. Bernadette asked: 'Will you have the goodness to put your name in writing?', and the apparition, speaking for the first time replied: 'That isn't necessary.' It then asked: 'Will you be kind enough to come here for a fortnight?' To which the child said 'Yes'. The figure spoke again. 'I don't promise to make you happy in this world, but in the next.' And then she disappeared. I should make it clear that the onlookers neither saw nor heard the figure, and only heard from Bernardette what had taken place when she emerged from her trance.

From this occasion on, Bernardette went to the grotto every single day until 4 March. While there had till now been disagreement as to whom the vision represented, Mme Milhet, one of the adults previously mentioned, had decided that it was probably the Virgin Mary; and that idea now became increasingly accepted. After the third vision, Bernardette started to refer to 'the lady' or 'the young lady'.

On 19 February her mother and Aunt Bernarde, the one with the bar, went with Bernardette to the grotto, the latter wearing a Miraculous Medal. No words were said, and the child's face during her ecstasy so shocked her mother Louise that she feared her daughter was about to die.

About the vision of 20 February, even the apparently authoritative accounts differ. Some claim that it was silent but Hellé[6] affirms that the lady taught Bernardette a secret prayer that was not in the catechism, and not a word of which she ever revealed. The trips to the grotto were being undertaken before 6 am each morning, and on the next morning up to a thousand people were there to see Bernardette's ecstasy. She was seen to start crying, and when asked why she explained that the lady had looked very sad, and had just said, 'Pray for sinners'. Later in the day Bernardette was subjected to two lengthy interviews, one with the local curate, the other with the Imperial Procurator, accompanied by the local Captain of Police. They appear to have approached their task with considerable cynicism, and to have questioned the child while she stood for over three hours. Despite threats and trickery, they do not seem to have found any significant contradiction or inconsistency in what she said. These upsets led Francois and Louise Soubirous to forbid their daughter to go to the grotto on the Monday morning. She duly went to school, but curiosity, or compulsion, got the better of her, and followed by police and about fifty members of the public (who presumably had waited by the school), she went anyway. There was no vision.

Six o'clock on the morning of the 23rd saw the grandest group of observers yet at the grotto, including a medical doctor and one Estrade, a tax inspector who was converted on the spot. There is some confusion as to exactly what the vision was reported to have said on this occasion. Neame[5] and Hellé[6] claim that three secrets were imparted to her (a constant element of the apparitions to children) with the command that, 'I forbid you to repeat this to anyone.' Other commentators are not so sure. The vision of the following day, the 24th, was the eighth in the series, and Bernardette was heard to call out, supposedly repeating what she had been told, 'Penitence, Penitence, Penitence!' Neame says she was told, 'You're to pray to God for sinners.'

It is surprising that even in this, the most famous Marian apparition, so little attention was paid to precise detail by the contemporary investigators. Information concerning speech, events, times and dates is missing, and in consequence the evidential value of some reports is severely handicapped. It is very difficult to establish the facts.

The next day, the 25th, is important, because it forms the basis of the healings in the Lourdes water that have become so famous over the years. Something over three hundred people attended the grotto on this day. Bernardette was seen to move from saying the rosary, suddenly scrambling on hands and knees into the grotto itself. She seemed to be searching the ground for something; then she started putting handfuls of earth in her mouth, and retching in consequence. She did this three or four times until she found mud rather than earth, then went and ate some leaves from a wild plant growing nearby. Her antics aroused both pity and horror among her observers, but later she explained that the lady had said, 'Go and drink at the spring and wash yourself in it.' She thought that the figure had meant the stream, but it had then pointed to the ground, and in the end the child had found the patch of damp earth. The lady had then said, 'Go and eat that plant there.' (No reason is given for this extraordinary instruction.)

It is one of the genuine, physical mysteries of Lourdes that from the scrabbling in the ground came forth a spring that two days later was producing more than eighteen gallons of water a day, and now forms the focal point of the shrine.

Incredibly, there is actually doubt as to whether or not an apparition took place on the next day, and there is doubt as to what, if anything, was said on the 27th. It may have been 'Go kiss the ground as a penance for sinners', and that was what the child appeared to do. She behaved similarly at what is generally counted as the eleventh vision, on 28 February.

There is some evidence that by the time of the next vision, the twelfth, on Monday 1 March 1858, the water from the spring was already being bottled, and that rumours of its curative powers were spreading in the district. If this is so, it is easy to imagine what effect this factor might have had upon Bernardette, particularly if she had heard the claim that one observer had been cured of paralysis in two fingers by her power or that of the water itself. The only remarkable part of this vision would appear to have been when Bernardette produced a rosary that a friend had left her. The lady spoke a little sharply, 'Where is your own rosary? That one is not yours. Use your own.'

The next day, however, it is possible to detect a new tone and approach creeping into the vision's dealings with Bernardette, and Bernardette's dealings with the authorities. Perhaps she had realized that if, like at La Salette, a healing spring could burst forth where there had been none before, she could also become the channel for messages of greater import than those hitherto transmitted. She said that she had been told, 'Go and tell the priests that people are to come here in procession.' She went straight off to pass the message on to Father Peyramale, the parish priest – who, incidentally, never once attended the grotto during the entire course of the visions. He responded with more anger than interest, and she went away, only to return later, saying that he was also 'to build a chapel here'. He was less than pleased.

If reports of the visions and their content do not actually agree on details, then it is quite hopeless to try to determine how many observers turned up at the grotto on any particular day. One hundred or one thousand on one day; 7000 or 20,000 on another. The figure used depends, it seems, on the author's degree of belief or disbelief. Anyway, there were some thousands of people present on the morning of 3 March, but there was no apparition then. A brief vision is said to have occurred in the afternoon, but in silence. An even larger crowd was present on the 4th, when some sort of miracle was widely expected, though none occurred. In the afternoon, after Bernardette had suffered considerable harrassment and annoyance from the crowd, she again went to try to convince Father Peyramale about the procession and the chapel. He, for his part, asked that the lady should name herself.

It will be recalled that early in the series of visions, Bernardette had felt herself called by an 'inner summons' to attend the grotto at particular times. Till now this had meant at least once a day at 6 am and often one later in the day too. A fairly predictable business. But next came a three-week break until 25 March, the Thursday in Passion Week, and the Feast of the Annunciation of the Virgin Mary. Then she was called again. By now the grotto was awash with flowers and candles.

Theologically speaking – to use a word that does not

A typical idealized interpretation of a Lourdes vision.

crop up much in writing about religious visions – 25
March 1858 has been treated as vital evidence of who,

precisely, had been appearing in the grotto; though many had, obviously, decided long since. I have mentioned, when speaking of Bernardette's stay at Bartres, why I am less than convinced by the supposed spontaneity of the message. And even if she had not heard the term at the Lagues household, then surely she must have done as her own popularity attracted believers from all over the countryside, many of whom wanted to talk to her and discuss the visions with her.

At the grotto on 25 March Bernardette asked the vision three times, 'Madame, will you kindly tell me who you are?' After the third request the lady unclasped her hands, 'and extended her arms, as portrayed in the miraculous medal'. She then replied, 'I am the Immaculate Conception.' She then vanished almost immediately.

Two more visions are said to have occurred before Bernardette's visitor went for ever. But neither occasion, 7 April or 16 July produced any message, though in her ecstasy on the former date Bernardette was observed to display a remarkable insensitivity to a candle flame playing on her fingers. The Lourdes visions were over; the Lourdes legend – sometimes a very different matter – had just begun.

FOUR:
'I only went to look at the sky'
PONTMAIN, FRANCE,
17 JANUARY 1871

It is hard for us, in the English-speaking world, to imagine just how horrific was the war of 1870-71 between France and Germany, or what an effect it had on the rest of Europe. Napoleon III had lost the Battle of Sedan in dramatic fashion in September 1870. Within months Strasbourg and Metz had fallen, and Paris was under the most fearful siege of the last two centuries. The French army had suffered severe losses, and morale was at its lowest. On the day of the vision at Pontmain, the German army was within a few miles of Laval, the centre of the diocese in which Pontmain lay and the chief town of the Mayenne.

Of the five hundred or so inhabitants of the village of Pontmain, thirty-eight had been conscripted into the army. One of them was a young man, August Friteau, and on the evening of 17 January 1871, good news regarding his safety had reached the village. At about half-past five, one Janette Detais, the village undertaker, arrived at the farm of Friteau's step-father, Cesar Barbadette, to pass the news on to him. He had been working with his two sons Eugene, age twelve, and Joseph, age ten, breaking down furze to make it edible for their horses; but when Detais arrived he paused to speak to her. Oddly enough, Eugene, who was Fritau's godson as well as his half-brother and of whom Friteau was apparently very fond, did not stop to listen to what she had to say but instead went to the open door of the barn. He is reported as saying later, 'I only went to look at the sky.'

Snow was still on the ground from when it had fallen in the morning. The sky was clear, and it was already dark. As he looked towards the next-door house, the early stages of this remarkable vision began.

Compared to most of the other major children's visions, there is relatively little source material about Pontmain, particularly in English. Most of the more modern accounts are very brief, so in the main I have compiled the following account from two earlier, more substantial reports. One is *The Apparition at Pontmain* by L'Abbé Richard,[7] translated into English as early as 5 August 1871, and published that same year. The other is a long section in *The Blessed Virgin in the Nineteenth Century*, by Bernard St John,[8] published in 1903. I have not, for whatever reason, found any account that does not accept the children's testimony as substantially authentic.

To return to the story. Eugene Barbadette is said to have spent about fifteen minutes undisturbed at the barn door. Initially, he noticed a 'lack of stars' over the roof of the nearby house. Then, suddenly, 'over the roof of that house', the vision itself commenced. Later in his life, when he had become a priest, he described what he saw in these terms:

I saw a woman of extraordinary beauty. She appeared to be young – about eighteen or twenty years of age – and tall of stature. She was clad in a garment of deep blue... Her dress was covered with gold stars, pentagonal in form, all of the same size and brilliant, but without emitting rays. They were not very numerous, and seemed to be scattered over the blue without regard to method. The blue garment was ample, showing certain strongly-marked folds, and without girdle or compression of any kind from the neck to the feet. The sleeves were ample and long, falling over the hands. On the feet, which the dress left uncovered, were *chaussons* of the same blue as the dress and ornamented with gold bows. On the head was a black veil half covering the forehead, concealing the hair and ears, and falling over the shoulders. Above this was a gold crown resembling a diadem, higher in front than elsewhere, and widening-out at the sides. A red line, from five to six millimetres wide encircled the crown at about the middle . . . the hands were small . . . the face was slightly oval . . . smiles of ineffable sweetness played about the mouth.

One report suggests that Eugene thought at first that the vision was a presentiment of the death of his soldier brother. Anyway, he spoke to no-one till Jeanne Detais

The four principal witnesses at Pontmain.

came out of the barn, when he asked her, 'Janette, look there over Augustin Guidecoq's house, and see if you can see anything?'

There is some variation in the reports in the distance at which the vision was seen – from twenty feet away, to a hundred metres away to six metres up in the air. Whichever it was, Jeanne Detais could see nothing out of the ordinary. But Eugene's father and brother had also heard what he had said and came to the door as well. His father, too, saw nothing; but when Eugene asked his brother if he could see anything he replied: 'Yes, I can see a beautiful lady.' 'How is she dressed?' asked Eugene. 'I see quite plainly a tall lady with a blue dress, with golden stars upon her dress, and blue slippers on, with gold bows upon them.'

If we are to believe this account, which dates from soon after the event, Joseph was further able to describe the vision, independently, but concurring with what his brother was seeing. The boys' father tried to convince them that they could see nothing, and the three of them set back to work, but his curiosity quickly got the better of him, and he sent Eugene back outside. When the boy reported that the lady was still there he was sent to fetch his mother. She came out to find Joseph clapping his hands in excitement but she, too, could not share in his experience. However, she was convinced enough to ensure that the children behaved in a proper manner, and had the family say five 'Our Fathers' and 'Hail Marys' in honour of the visitor. She may have taken the initiative thereby in providing a positive identification.

By this time the neighbours were showing an interest. The boys' parents passed it off as nothing, but continued their devotions in the barn with the door shut. At 6.15 it was supper time, and the work was finished; the boys went reluctantly into the house. They rushed their food, and went back outside yet again. When they returned they said, 'It is just the same. The Lady is as tall as Sister Vataline.' The Sister was one of the nuns who ran the village school, and she stood about 5 feet 6 inches. At the mention of her name the boys' mother, who could not make up her mind whether they were lying, or whether they should continue with their prayers, decided that Sister Vitaline must be sent for.

A number of children were still at the school with the Sister, and they no doubt heard Victoire Barbadette explain that her sons had seen something, but that she herself could not see it. There is no telling just what details she may have mentioned in her haste and excitement; she may well have said that the vision was of the Virgin herself. Initially, just Sister Vitaline went to the barn. She seems to have been able to see the three stars that the boys said framed the Virgin's head, but no more than that. The story goes that these three stars were never seen again by the villagers.

The Sister and Victoire Barbadette returned to the school, and this time the three children went while their teacher stayed. Of the three girls two, Francoise Richer, age eleven, and Jeanne-Marie Lebosse, age nine, are reported to have joined in the chorus of recognition as soon as they arrived where Eugene and Joseph still stood gazing, saying, 'O, what a beautiful lady.' The third, Augustine Manton, whose age I cannot ascertain, saw nothing.

In the meantime, Sister Vitaline had returned with her colleague, Sister Marie Edouard. She spoke to the four children, though no vision was apparent to her, and, perceptively, is supposed to have said: 'As these children see, we must bring some more that are younger.'

Making her actions suit her words, she called at the home of the six-year-old Eugene Friteau, who was carried by his grandmother to the scene, while she went on to the home of the parish-priest, Abbé Guerin. Enthusiastically, she arrived exclaiming: 'There is a prodigy – an apparition – the children can see the Blessed Virgin.' Not surprisingly, the old and well-respected priest went quickly to the barn, accompanied by his housekeeper. He too was not party to the vision, but just after he arrived the six-year-old Eugene Friteau also made it plain that he could see the lady; however he was a weak and ill child, with only three months to live. He was taken home. There was also a claim that Augustine Boitin, the daughter of the villager cobbler, shared in the vision. But as she was only two, and her only verbal response was to say 'Jesus, Jesus', we cannot make much of her testimony.

It is very unfortunate that nobody seems to have kept an accurate record of the passage of time, for now the sequence of events enters its climatic phase. It appears that by now between fifty and sixty people, of all ages, were standing by the barn, including the priest and the two nuns, one of whom was reciting out loud a rather obscure religious devotion, the Rosary of the Japanese Martyrs. The four witnesses, two boys and two girls, were the centre of attention, and the others were crowded around them, asking them what they could see. I suspect that the sort of interest and pressure they were now experiencing may well have had some effect on the development of the vision. The images that now begin to appear are reminiscent of traditional themes in religious art, and particularly of the Miraculous Medal, The content, however, may be a different matter.

It was soon after the arrival of the priest that the first change in the vision was reported. A small red cross appeared on the Virgin's chest, then an oval 'frame' appeared around her, with four unlit candles within it. The children then reported that the lady had begun to 'look sad', so the priest instructed the crowd to say the rosary together. As those present knelt, so the children said that the figure had grown to eleven or twelve feet in height, the frame expanding with its growth, almost as if it grew strength from the devotion. To quote from the 1871 account:

The stars of the sky appeared to the children to move, and form in order before the lady, and arrange themselves two and two beneath the feet, like people standing one each side when a carriage is passing by. At the same time the stars on her robe increased in number.

As Sister Marie-Edouard started singing the *Magnificat*, another change took place.

A large white surface, about a yard and a half broad, and about twelve yards long, appeared below the lady's feet and the blue oval. It seemed to the children as if an invisible hand was slowly forming beautiful letters in gold upon this tablet, or paper.

Gradually, the children said, the word 'MAIS' (but) appeared, and remained for about ten minutes, during which time news arrived at the village that the Prussians were at Laval. More words appeared, the whole eventually reading: 'MAIS PRIEZ MES ENFANTS' (But pray, my children). Interestingly enough, beginning a sentence with the ungrammatical 'Mais' was a habit of Sister Vitaline's.

By now the time was about half-past seven, some two hours after the vision began. It had become so cold that the crowd went inside the barn, and the four children stood in the doorway, reporting to the rest what they could see. Sister Marie Edouard began the Litany of Loretto (the site of the miracle of the Holy House) and

The barn at Pontmain, after alterations.

the children spelt out more words. This time they were: 'DIEU VOUS EXAUCERA EN PEU DE TEMPS' (God will soon answer your prayers). The crowd immediately assumed that the message referred to the course of the war, and said so out loud. The children reported that the lady's response was to laugh. Now a second line of writing began to appear, as the singing and worship continued. It read: 'MON FILS SE LAISSE TOUCHER' (My son allows himself to be moved).

The crowd, now more excited than ever, began a hymn to the Virgin, and by the end of it the words had disappeared. In front of the lady appeared a red cross, about eighteen inches high, on which was an image of Christ in the same colour. A smaller, upper crossbar bore the words 'Jesus Christ'. The lady held it out in her hands till the whole cross vanished, and she smiled again. A star moved round within the frame, lighting the candles, before coming to rest above the lady's head.

Abbé Guerin called the crowd to say their night prayers together; it was about half-past eight. To quote the children in the 1871 report,

A large white veil, rising from beneath the feet of the Blessed Virgin and slowly going up, had covered her as far up as her waist. Rising up farther by degrees, it surrounded her up to her neck. Eugene said it seemed as though she had gone in to a kind of bag. The children could now see only the face of the lady, full of heavenly beauty, and still smiling. Soon, however, her face was concealed, the crown alone remaining visible with the star above it; and then all disappeared, with the large blue oval and the four tapers which had remained lighted till the end. The parish priest called to the children from the farther end of the barn, where he was seated, and said to them:

'Do you see anything still?'

And they answered all together, 'No, reverend sir, all has disappeared. It is all over.'

It was a quarter to nine o'clock. The crowd went slowly home, talking together of an event so prodigious, and which left an impression of sweetness, profound and ineffaceable.

It is claimed that the German Army halted its advance on Laval at 5.30 pm on 17 January 1871, the very time and date of the commencement of the Pontmain vision. Certainly, it does appear to have been on that evening that the decision was made. I have actually seen it written that General Schmidt, the Prussian commander, said the next morning: 'We cannot go farther. Yonder, in the direction of Brittany, there is an invisible Madonna barring the way.'

There is no reason to believe this last item; it shows every sign of being a touch of exaggeration on what is already a rather remarkable story. For even if the channel of communication was not the real Virgin Mary, but more an amalgamation of the Holy Mother, Sister Vitaline, and the Miraculous Medal, we still have four or five peasant children in an obscure village displaying some knowledge of complex and distant events to a large number of their relatives and neighbours. Of course, if the vision not only reported, but caused, the retreat of the German Army, the Pontmain vision becomes an even greater mystery.

FIVE:
'I went out then, and ran up to see what was to be seen'
KNOCK, IRELAND, 21 AUGUST 1879

By now, having looked closely at three visionary events in the same country, spread over twenty-five years, there is no doubt that something of a pattern is beginning to develop. The witnesses: rural background, poor standard of living, little education or experience of the world. The vision: moving, speaking, to all intents and purposes alive – often communicating information concerning current, even future, matters in a world unknown to the young witnesses.

Assessing the evidence for the visions would be much easier if they all conformed to this sort of pattern – and many, actually, do, though there may be a number of reasons for that. But even some cases that have led to considerable fame for the witnesses, to pilgrimage, and to reports of healing miracles, appear to follow an entirely different sequence, and Knock is one of them. Because of frequent criticisms of this case it is particularly important to use the most direct and original accounts of the events that are available, and in this we are very fortunate to have transcripts (in what I believe to be perfectly sound translation) of the witness reports collected by the First Commission of Enquiry into the apparitions, set up only six months after the events. I shall quote extensively from these reports.

Knock is now a centre of international pilgrimage

and an airport is at present being constructed there to bring visitors from all over the world. When Pope John Paul II visited Ireland he went to Knock. With the exception of Lourdes, it is undoubtedly the most popular shrine arising from a vision in Europe. But how did it come to be so? It is certain that the early claims of healing associated with the vision played a vital part in publicizing and establishing Knock in the early years, but what of the evidence for the apparition itself?

Knock was just a small village in County Mayo, in the West of Ireland, remote and undistinguished by anything but the vision. In 1879 it was an ardently nationalist district, though it had suffered less badly from the horrors of the famine and of absentee English landlords

The chapel at Knock.

than had many other villages in the area. This is not to say that the people of the village were not poor – most of them were; but there had been little of the real suffering that the middle years of the century had seen in much of the rest of Ireland.

The event that is claimed to have happened at Knock is an extraordinary one indeed, even compared to the others we have already considered. It took place on the flat gable-end of the village church, on a Thursday evening, 21 August 1879. It seems to have begun before dusk fell, and continued into the hours of darkness. It was seen, apparently, by fifteen witnesses, though one of these was only eleven, one eight, and one five. As I have mentioned, the eye-witness reports come from the records and findings of the First Commission of Enquiry set up by Dr John McHale, the Archbishop of Tuam, at the end of September 1879.

The first witness to what may perhaps be better termed an apparition than a vision was Mary McLoughlin, the housekeeper to Archdeacon Cavanagh, the village priest (who, oddly enough, steadfastly refused all requests to go and see the vision but later, probably for reasons of political pragmatism, expressed his full approval of them). Her age is uncertain, but she was about forty-five years old at the time. She had walked by the chapel at 7 pm while it was still quite light:

On passing by the chapel, and at a little distance from it, I saw a wonderful number of strange figures or appearances at the gable, one like the Blessed Virgin Mary, and one like St Joseph, another a bishop; I saw an alter.

I was wondering to see there such an extraordinary group; yet I passed on and said nothing, thinking that possibly the Archdeacon had been supplied with these beautiful figures from Dublin, or somewhere else, and that he had said nothing about them, but left them in the open air; I saw a white light about them; I thought the whole thing strange.

Strangely, as it seems to me, she then walked on to the

home of one Mary Beirne, where she passed half an hour. The two were on their way back to the Archdeacon's house when Beirne exclaimed, 'Look at the beautiful figures!'

McLoughlin told her to go and fetch her mother, brother, sister, and niece, and she set off to do so. In the meantime, Mary McLoughlin watched the scene till Mary Beirne returned with the first group of relatives, only to go off and find more. Mary McLoughlin described the scene she then saw as follows. It is clear that once night fell, the images became clearer:

It was about a quarter past eight o'clock, and beginning to be quite dark. The sun had set; it was raining at the time. I beheld on this occasion, not only the three figures, but an altar further on the left of the figure of the Blessed Virgin Mary, and to the left of the bishop and above the altar a lamb about the size of that which is five weeks old. Behind the lamb appeared the cross; it was away a bit from the lamb, while the latter stood in front from it, and not resting on the wood of the cross. Around the Lamb a number of gold-like stars appeared in the form of a halo. This altar was placed right under the window of the gable and more to the east of the figures, all, of course, outside the church at Knock.

It is clear that as Mary Beirne did the rounds of her relatives, she prepared them for what she expected them to see. This is hardly surprising considering the excitement of the moment; but we must consider the evidence of the others, bearing a possible predisposition to a miraculous event in mind. Her mother gave a valuable report to the Commission:

I went out immediately and came to the spot indicated. When I arrived there I saw distinctly the three figures. I went in immediately to kiss, as I thought, the feet of the Blessed Virgin; but felt nothing in my embrace but the wall, and I wondered why I could not feel with my hands the figures which I had so plainly and distinctly seen.

The three figures appeared motionless, statue-like; they were standing by the gable of the church in the background, and seemed raised about two feet above the ground. The Blessed Virgin was in the centre; she was clothed in white, and covered in what appeared to be one white garment; her hands were raised to the same position as that in which a priest holds his hands when praying at holy Mass. I remarked distinctly the lower portions of her feet, and kissed them three times; she had on her head something resembling a crown, and her eyes were turned up heavenwards.

It was raining very heavily at the time, but no rain fell where the figures were. I felt the ground carefully with my hands, and it was perfectly dry. The wind was blowing from the south, right against the gable of the chapel, but no rain fell on that portion of the gable or chapel in which the figures were. There was no movement or active sign of life about the figures . . .

Bridget Trench was about seventy-five years old at the time she made this statement, and it does seem to be a sound piece of observation, with a degree of spontaneous, but practical experiment. She also saw the other two figures but nothing, it seems, of the lamb, cross, or altar. It is very hard to accept, in the light of this report, that any of the figures had any physical substance.

Already, we appear to have some very different perceptions of the apparition. The testimony of Mary Beirne herself is even more detailed. She commences her account by telling how she noticed three figures 'standing out' from the gable, and that the figures appeared to be 'The Blessed Virgin, St Joseph, and St John'. She continued:

That of the Blessed Virgin was life-size, the others apparently either not so big or not so high as her figure; they stood a little distance out from the gable wall, and as well as I could judge, a foot and a half or two from the ground. The Virgin stood erect, with eyes raised to heaven, her hands elevated to the shoulders or a little higher, the palms inclined slightly towards the shoulders or bosom; she wore a large cloak of a white colour, hanging in full folds and somewhat loosely around her shoulders, and fastened to the neck; she wore a crown on the head – rather a large crown – and it appeared to be somewhat yellower than the dress or robes worn by Our Blessed Lady. In the figure of St Joseph, the head was slightly bent, and inclined towards the Blessed Virgin, as if paying her respect; it represented the saint somewhat aged, with grey whiskers and greyish hair.

The third figure appeared to be that of St John the Evangelist; I do not know, only I thought so, except the fact that at one time I saw a statue at the chapel of Lekanvey, near Westport, County Mayo, very much resembling the figure which now stood before me . . .

Above the altar, and resting on it, was a lamb, standing with the fact towards St John, thus fronting the western sky. I saw no cross or crucifix. On the body of the lamb and around it, I saw golden stars, or small brilliant lights, glittering like jets or glass balls, reflecting the light of some luminous body. I remained from a quarter past eight to half past nine o'clock. At the time it was raining.

It is unfortunate – surprising, even – that only this one group of family and friends, all associates of Mary Beirne, witnessed the events at close quarters. The only external, independent confirmation comes from a man of sixty-five who was some 800 yards from the church:

My name is Patrick Walsh; I live at Ballinderrig, an English mile from the chapel of Knock. I remember well the 21st August, 1879. It was a very dark night. It was raining heavily. About nine o'clock on that night, I was going on some business through my land, and standing at a distance of about half a mile from the chapel. I saw a very bright light on the southern gable-end of the chapel; it appeared to be a large globe of golden light; I never saw, I thought, so brilliant a light before; it appeared high up in the air and around the chapel gable, and it was circular in its appearance; it was quite stationary, and it seemed to retain the same brilliancy all through. The following day I made enquiries in order to learn if there were any lights seen in the place that night; it was only then I heard of the Vision or Apparition that the people had seen.

This lack of publicity seems to me to require an explanation. Surely, a small Catholic village would have speedily been put into a state of great excitement, with all who could walk jostling for position to see what would surely have been regarded as a miracle. Within half an hour, the news would have reached those less than a mile away, like Patrick Walsh. Before the evening was out I would have expected the inhabitants of neighbouring villages to have been pouring into Knock, at least to see what all the fuss was about. And if the Priest, Archdeacon Cavanagh, had given any credence at all to the story his housekeeper told him, surely he would have run to see what was going on at his own church?

Whatever the explanation, none of this happened, and instead the group of friends and relatives stood for much of the evening, apparently making no effort to share their experience. Answers would be easier to come by, and the evidence for the Knock apparition considerably stronger, had outsiders been involved; but they were not. As we have only the testimony of this group, it is to them we must return in the hope of further clarification: firstly to Mary Beirne's brother Dominick, aged between eighteen and twenty, who is the first to mention the departure of the apparition:

I then went with her (Mary Beirne) and by this time some ten or twelve people had been collected around the place, namely the ditch or wall fronting the gable, where the vision was being seen, and to the south of the schoolhouse; then I beheld the three likenesses or figures that have been already described – the Blessed Virgin, St Joseph, and St John, as my sister called the bishop, who was like one preaching, with his hands raised towards the shoulder, and the forefinger and middle finger pointedly set... the eyes of the images could be seen; they were like figures, inasmuch as they did not speak.

I was filled with wonder at the sight I saw; I was so affected that I shed tears; I continued looking on for fully an hour, and then I went away to visit Mrs Campbell, who was in a dying state; when we returned the vision had disappeared.

Next, the testimony of his younger sister Margaret, aged twenty-one:

Shortly after, about eight o'clock, my niece, Catherine Murray, called me out to see the Blessed Virgin and the other saints that were standing at the south gable of the chapel. I went out then, and ran up to see what was to be seen. I there beheld the Blessed Virgin with a bright crown on her head, and St Joseph to her right, his head inclined a little towards Our Blessed Lady, and St John the Evangelist to her left, eastward, holding in his left hand a book of the gospels, and his right hand raised the while, as if in the attitude of preaching to the people who stood before him at the ditch. The Virgin appeared with hands uplifted as if in prayer, with eyes turned towards heaven, and wearing a lustrous crown. I saw an altar there; it was surrounded with a bright light, nay, with a light at times sparkling, and so too were the other figures, which were similarly surrounded.

Taken together, these reports more or less cover all the features mentioned by the other witnesses in their testimony. Dominick Beirne Senior, aged thirty-six, and Patrick Hill, aged eleven, mention that the Virgin wore white robes. Hill was again interviewed in 1897, when he went into great, and not altogether credible, detail about a rose in Mary's crown, St John's bare feet, and angels with wings that fluttered for over ninety minutes, but did not turn their faces to him! Patrick Beirne, aged sixteen, whose testimony is given mostly in report form rather that in the first person, is actually quoted as saying in 1879 that: 'I remained only ten minutes, and then I went away' – incredible behaviour, surely, for a young man in the company of close relatives supposedly witnessing the most astonishing sight of his life?

Two Commissions of Enquiry were held: one in 1879, and the second as late as 1936. The first interviewed fifteen witnesses, but of these only two survived to the second: Mary Beirne (latterly O'Connell) and Patrick Beirne. The first Commission was not, it appears, either sceptical or too demanding, and even included the Knock parish priest. The second seems to have been more thorough, and in 1936, too, the Knock Medical Bureau was founded. While the many claims of healing at, or because of, Knock were responsible for much of its present fame, there is little doubt that many of the miracles claimed before this date were of dubious authenticity, and that the cures could well have been explained by a number of other factors.

The Knock apparition has always aroused great passion in both its critics and its supporters. The European style of aggressive investigation has usually involved the interrogation of witnesses by the civil authorities, and while it is easy to sympathize with the young children who underwent such an investigation, it is interesting to speculate what the Knock witnesses would have said in a similar situation. However, such investigative techniques were not applied in this case and in consequence, there has been extensive speculation since very shortly after the events.

Because the Church authorities discouraged it, no press report of the vision appeared till four months later; yet the news had travelled by word of mouth through the Catholic world long before this. Shortly after the first press reports various forms of light phenomena were allegedly seen in and around Knock, but there is no reason to take these seriously. Most of the early documentary evidence suggests that even the ecclesiastical authorities were sceptical; but the accounts of the First Commission unfortunately show no sign of any detailed examination of witnesses, or of any attempt to reconcile the variations and inconsistencies between the testimonies that were presented. Was there an altar; a lamb; a cross? Were there glittering stars, or not? But then, as we have found at both Lourdes and Pontmain, not everybody is a witness to the same thing; and this is also true of many cases in the paranormal and psychic research fields. Knock is far from being unique in this respect.

Certainly, there seems to have been something of an 'establishment versus the common people' air about the

Knock apparition for many years. Within a few months of the first media reports there was hardly a bed to be had for the pilgrims who were now visiting the village in increasing numbers. The fee for being allowed to sleep in an armchair in one of the village houses was one shilling and sixpence – a large amount of money in 1879. It is plain that the apparitions brought substantial commercial opportunities and advantages to the village, and these continue to date, to the discomfort of some more conservative commentators.

David Berman, a lecturer in Philosophy at Dublin University, wrote an article that appeared in *The Irish Times* in 1979. In it, he reached the conclusion that there were four possible explanations for what is said to have happened at Knock on the evening of 21 August 1879. These, he said, were:

1. That the Virgin Mary actually appeared.
2. That there was a mass hallucination.
3. That there was collusion and conspiracy among the witnesses.
4. That there was some kind of hoax.

I would agree with Berman in confidently dismissing options (2) and (3). The report of Patrick Walsh from half a mile away, if true, makes mass hallucination highly unlikely; and the obvious candour and patent inconsistency of the tales told by the witnesses to the First Commission argue strongly against both options. With regard to the first option, I will delay giving an opinion till the end of this book – Berman's words 'The Virgin Mary actually appeared' themselves raise a great many questions. But the fourth option is one that has been taken very seriously over the years, and we must consider it before moving on to the more esoteric wonders of Fatima.

The term 'hoax' here means a hoax *on* the witnesses, not *by* them. It comes down to two choices, both of which have been put forward, and generally dismissed, many times since the event occurred. The first choice is highly unlikely, and involves the creation by an unknown artist of high skill of a lifesize and lifelike work of delicate and complex art on the outside wall of the church, without anyone noticing. Not only this, but the painting would have to have been done in just the one medium, a primitive luminous, phosphorescent paint, *and* would have had to have been removed before dark the next night. Clearly, this is not a viable proposition. However, the second 'hoax' explanation has to be taken seriously. It entails the possible use of a magic lantern.

There is no doubt that there were, in 1879, makes of magic lantern available in Ireland that could have thrown an image of the size and brightness recorded at Knock. And to judge from some contemporary advertisements that I have seen quoted, statues and statuary were just about the ideal subject matter for such a device; images of statues cast by a magic lantern could look very real indeed. Now, there are strong arguments against this hypothesis, particularly in that there seems to have been no building situated nearby that would have been at all suitable for the concealment of a magic lantern and its operator. Also, I would imagine that the observers would have cast shadows on to the gable-end as they stood between it and the light-source. There is no evidence that this happened. Similarly, the witnesses were apparently of normal intelligence. Might they not have been able to detect such a hoax, had one occurred?

In the *Irish Times* article, Berman makes a number of very valid points in support of the likelihood of the 'magic lantern' explanation, referring particularly to the increase in the brightness of the images as darkness fell. Other details he mentions include:

1. The figures were motionless.
2. They appeared to be statues.
3. They were intangible.
4. They appeared up against a flat gable wall, a foot or two from the ground.

5. They embodied iconographic conventions.
6. They were surrounded by light.

All these arguments remain valid, and taken together are convincing; if it were not for the lack of a likely perch for the hoaxer and his equipment, it would be hard not to accept this explanation as correct.

However, it is not as simple as that. There was a rumour that a local policeman had actually operated the magic lantern, but this seems never to have been satisfactorily followed up. The facts do not really fit snugly together in detail, and there must have been some misperception, at least. In the end we have for evidence only the sort of testimonies that we have already quoted, and any judgements will have to be made on that basis.

In her careful, but undoubtedly approving, account in *A Woman Clothed with the Sun*,[9] Mary Purcell, an established Catholic author, gives the Blessed Virgin at Knock the title, 'The Lady of Silence', and says:

The very silence of the apparition is an invitation to ponder the symbolism of the altar with the Lamb and the Cross, the position and demeanour of the three figures . . . It is helpful, when thinking of Knock, to remember that messages can be conveyed without the aid of either the spoken or the written word. A mother's gesture, her glance, her demeanour, her very silence, say much to her attentive children. At Knock, the Blessed Mother, reverent, silent, adoring, showed how to pray.

The central problem of assessing Knock is, indeed, that it was a vision without either speech or motion; any identification depended on the existing knowledge and experience of the witnesses; there was no kind of verification from the vision itself. Had it not been for the many consequent healings and conversions, I cannot imagine that Knock would have achieved its present fame. Similarly, the village and the area would not have benefited from the sound commercial and political instincts that still cause Knock to prosper to this day. It is Knock, more than any other case, that emphasizes the problem of separating the event from the legend.

SIX:

'Will you take all three of us to heaven soon?'

FATIMA, PORTUGAL, 1915, 1916 AND 1917

Until I started researching the Fatima events in depth I had thought that the subject was, if not exactly simple, at least straightforward. A series of visions, yes, such as made Lourdes a little complicated and hard to analyse; with Beauraing, we will find similar problems, and Garabandal could well overwhelm the casual reader with quantity and detail. But with Fatima it appeared that there were only the six visions to be dealt with, in addition to the fascinating links with many other areas of paranormal experience that derive from the floating balls of light in the earlier visions, and the aerial phenomena in the last, that have become known as the 'Dance of the Sun'. Of course, I had heard a little of the prophecies supposedly made by the Virgin Mary, but on the whole this seemed to be one case that could just be told as a piece of history, and analysed on the basis that it was authentic.

This initial impression was only confirmed by the fact that with the possible exception of Lourdes, the shrine at Fatima is the most visited by Popes and senior Churchmen. Support for the authenticity of the visions, and the value of the content of the messages, has been lent by the most conservative areas of the Catholic Church. To a great many ordinary Catholics, the 'solar miracle' is a manifest-ation of the power of the almighty God, and of the willingness of Christ's Mother to intervene in human affairs.

Nothing about Fatima has turned out to be in the least bit simple or straightforward at all. Indeed, I have never seen such a collection of contradictory accounts of a case in any of the research I have done in the past ten years. Part of the problem is that very little was written about Fatima before the end of the Second World War, and most of the Catholic commentaries seem to date from after 1950. Thirty years later is not an ideal time to start writing about any event. Also, much of the original material, published at the same time as the visions, has become confused with the content of Lucia Santos' memoirs, which were only published in 1942. More of these later. The most important difficulty of all, though, is one that arises in a number of cases, but is most strongly emphasized in this instance. To put it briefly, the key point to remember about Fatima is that it was only the three children – and often only one of the three – that saw the Virgin Mary, or heard what she had to say. For all but the light phenomena, and the 'solar miracle', the only evidence we have is that of three young children, living through the most unsettled and extraordinary phase of their lives.

Young the children certainly were. Lucia Santos – always the leader and catalyst of the group, who was, in the course of time, to orchestrate the behaviour of vast crowds – was born on 22 March 1907. She was regarded as an unattractive child, but was capable, talkative, and alert. The other two children were her first cousins, Francisco and Jacinta Marto. Francisco, born on 11 June 1908, was affectionate and pleasant, though not particularly bright. Jacinta was born on 11 March 1910, and was pretty and sensitive; at times, she seems to have been very scared by the crowds that attended the later visions. All three children were from poor but respectable homes and reasonably devout Catholic backgrounds. All three were occupied in caring for the sheep that belonged to their families.

As has been stated, it is difficult to find any two accounts of the visions of May and June 1917 that agree in detail. However, it was at about midday on 13 May 1917 that the first vision took place. The children were grazing the sheep on a piece of land owned by Lucia's parents at the Cova da Iria, a natural amphitheatre about five hundred yards wide. It seems that the children had eaten and had just said the rosary together, quite possibly actually kneeling to do so. Suddenly, it is said, there was a flash, or flashes, of lightning and a brilliantly white lady appeared, either in the branches of a holm-oak tree, or

The Fatima witnesses: Jacinto, Francisco and Lucia.

possibly standing on a fern! There are contradictions in the accounts of this vision, and it is impossible that all the accounts are true. Some have Francisco seeing and hearing nothing at all; others have him seeing and not hearing. There are inconsistencies with regard to Jacinta as well. We only have Lucia's account of what happened, and have to accept that at face value. We can know nothing of what the other children felt or experienced, but as they became positively involved at this stage, presumably there must have been some basis for their later actions.

Lucia heard the 'girl' as they first described her, say, 'I come from Heaven', and, 'I have come to ask you to be here six times running at the same time on the thirteenth of each month. In October I will tell you who I am and what I want.'

As always seems to be the case, the reports soon received publicity. When the children returned to the Cova on 13 June, about sixty people were with them, and Lucia was seen to take the initiative. As the three of them recited the rosary she cried out, 'The Lady's coming', and the three children ran down to the holm-oak where the previous vision had been seen. The only independent report is that, as Lucia said the lady was leaving, the branches of the oak moved, 'as though her dress had trailed over them'. The dialogue with the Virgin was reported by Lucia soon after the event:

Lucia: You asked me to come back here, my lady, what do you want of me?

The Vision: I desire you to learn to read so that I can tell you what I want.

Lucia asked for the cure of a sick person whom one of her mother's neighbours had recommended to her.

The Vision: If he is converted, he will be cured within the course of the year.

Lucia: Will you take all three of us to Heaven soon?

The first of what have become known as the 'Secrets of Fatima' was given in reply to this last question:

The Vision; Yes, I shall soon come to take Jacinta and Francisco. But you must remain longer here below. Jesus wishes to use you in making me known and loved. I wish to spread devotion to my Immaculate Heart throughout the world.

She was not inaccurate; assuming, that is – and it is very hard to tell now – that the prophecy was actually released before the event. Francisco died in the influenza epidemic that followed the First World War, on 4 April 1919. This was one day after taking his first communion, and he was only ten years old. Jacinta died on 20 February 1920, from an attack of pleurisy that followed the influenza. She was only nine. This only emphasizes how very young these two were at the time of the visions.

Before 13 July and the third vision came round, a little barrier with a gate was built round the holm-oak, which was by now a centre of some devotion. Lucia had been criticized and called a liar and an associate of the devil. Life had not been easy for her, or her family. There were 5000 people present and they watched as Lucia again broke off in the middle of her prayers and shouted out loud. Again, the others followed her example, and though Jacinta was heard to encourage her to speak, Lucia did all the talking to the vision, asking for favours and miracles that friends and neighbours had asked her to pass on. However, the important words, as Lucia recounted them afterwards, were:

Lucia: Who are you? Will you tell me your name and work a miracle so that everyone will believe?

The Vision: Continue to come here every month. In October I shall tell you who I am and what I want. In October I shall work a great miracle so that everyone will believe you.

Lucia also reported a horrifying vision of hell, and a number of prophecies relating to Russia and the end of the war. But it seems that none of this predates 1942, and its evidential value is therefore very limited. A handful of witnesses reported seeing a white cloud round the children, and that the sun dimmed as the lady left.

On 13 August there were some 20,000 people waiting for the children at the Cova, but the children had been taken by force to Ourem, a nearby town, by the sub-prefect of the area. He held them there till the fifteenth of the month, questioning them once in the town hall and once in the prison. In the absence of the children, no vision of the Virgin was seen, but there were reports that at the time the visions had previously occurred some people heard thunder, saw a flash of light in the sky, and observed a small cloud form above the tree, which hung there for about ten minutes. Only a very small proportion of the crowd saw anything untoward.

On 19 August a compensatory vision was witnessed by the children at nearby Valinhos. Lucia said that she had seen the warning flash of light and sent one Joao, a boy who witnessed nothing, to fetch Jacinta who was nearby. The Virgin asked that a chapel should be built and also said, referring to the children's interrogation: 'Because of the unbelief of the free thinkers, the miracle promised for October will be less striking. But you will have to go to the Cova da Iria on the thirteenth of the two following months. Will you promise me that once more?' The children cut off the branch of the tree on which the lady's feet had been resting, and took it home. It was said to smell of a heavenly perfume.

With the fifth apparition, on 13 September 1917, before 25,000-30,000 people, we find our subject matter taking two definite courses. On the one hand, there are UFO-type phenomena witnessed by others besides the children, and on the other there is the vision of the Virgin. Many of those present saw nothing at all, but among those who did was Father Joao Quaresma, later to become Vicar-General of Leiria, the diocese in which Fatima lay:

To my great astonishment . . . I saw, clearly and distinctly, a luminous globe coming from the east and moving to the west, gliding slowly and majestically through space. With my hand I motioned to Monsignor Gois who was standing next to me, and who had been making fun of me for coming. Looking up he too had the good fortune to see this unexpected vision.

Suddenly this globe, giving off an extraordinary light, disappeared from my sight and Monsignor Gois, also, saw it no longer. But there was a little girl near us, dressed like Lucia and of about the same age, who continued to cry happily, 'I see it, I see it! Now it's coming down towards the bottom of the hill.'

It was, in fact, a luminous globe and, according to the assertions of those who saw it, oval in form with 'the widest part underneath – a sort of celestial airplane'.

As far as the vision itself was concerned, little was said. Lucia and her lady spoke more of the building of a chapel and the lady, so Lucia said, promised to return in October with St Joseph and the child Jesus. As she left, flowers – or petals at least – appeared to fall from nowhere in particular, a phenomenon also associated with a number of UFO reports. Once again, Lucia had initiated and conducted all the aspects of the event.

The miracle of 13 October had long been predicted, hoped for, prayed for. On the day, some 70,000 people crowded into the wide natural amphitheatre round the holm-oak in the Cova, and there is no doubt that the crowd was alive with expectation. It seems unlikely, however, that any of them anticipated what is actually said to have happened, and a good many of them saw nothing unusual at all. The events at Fatima on 13 October 1917, as well as being the most famous miraculous events of this century by common repute, are also the most intriguing of anomalous phenomena left without explanation. Oddly enough, the vision of the Virgin of that date has been largely ignored in the rush to investigate the so-called solar miracle.

The three children had difficulty in reaching the holm-oak through the massive crowd, and Jacinta was thoroughly unnerved. However, they fought their way through the forest of umbrellas (it was pouring with rain). Once in place, Lucia ordered that the umbrellas should be put away. Exactly at noon, she said that she had seen the flash, and then the vision. A few words were exchanged, closing with the Virgin saying: 'Men must correct their faults and ask pardon for their sins, in order that they no longer offend our Lord, who is already too much offended.' She then said goodbye to the children, and as she went Lucia (and possibly the other two children as well, depending on which accounts are followed) saw the whole holy family appear by the sun in the sky. Because of this she called out, 'Look at the sun', and the crowd duly did so.

There are a number of strange features about what happened next, and it is almost impossible to extract the facts from the mass of tales that have been handed down. I cannot see that one can categorically deny that something utterly remarkable took place at Fatima on that day; but against this there are many factors that prevent us drawing the simple conclusion that a divinely-inspired miracle took place.

Firstly, there were many representatives of the press present at the Cova, both journalists and photographers. There are many photographs of the crowd witnessing the vision; but in spite of the presence of cameras there is no photograph of the event that is even vaguely authentic; the one usually presented is actually of a solar eclipse in another part of the world, taken some time before 1917. What were the photographers doing? How could anyone miss a scoop like that?

Secondly, it is clear that only a proportion of the crowd, probably less than half, actually witnessed the miracle. There is some evidence to the effect that only those who were standing in a broad band across the centre of the Cova saw the vision; but the truth of this is now impossible to establish.

Thirdly, the accounts of the miracle, of the 'dance of the sun', are simply not consistent. It is not surprising that perception and memory should become clouded and

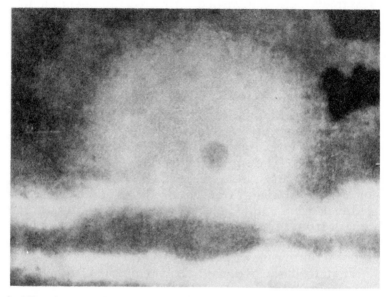

The photograph often presented as the solar miracle at Fatima.

uncertain in the face of such a wholly incomprehensible event; but these contradictions must raise some doubts as to the objective nature of what was seen.

One thing is sure – the sun did not move on that day, and there was no solar phenomenon that could account for the reports. No observatory or other body responsible for astronomical observation anywhere in the world reported anything the least bit unusual. There was no geophysical effect, no change in the tides. Whatever the object seen was, it seems to have been imbued with the purpose of affecting only the crowd at the Cova da Iria, and a few isolated observers further off. It does not seem to have been massive or, so far as I can tell, substantial. It may be safer to say of it that 'it happened', rather than that 'it was there'.

In a way, the 'solar miracle' accounts do not really belong in this book: they are not visions of the Virgin, and the connections between the two events at Fatima are less than clearly established. However, this phenomenon, or series of related phenomena, constitutes the only external, objective evidence of a supernatural event related to any of the visions. It is the only occasion on which the massive crowds of adults attending the site of a vision have had an experience related to that of the central, child witness. As such, it is an important part of our evidence overall.

There are surprisingly few convincing accounts of the solar event at Fatima, and most of them are seldom encountered. The earliest collection of them that I have been able to find is in an American book, *Fatima: the Facts*, by John De Marchi,[18] translated from the Portuguese and published in 1950. There is not space here to quote at length from the accounts given in this book, but I have selected a few examples of apparently responsible witness reports on that most peculiar day.

First, from the two major daily papers in Lisbon. *O Dia* reported:

At one o'clock in the afternoon, midday by the sun, the rain stopped. The sky, pearly grey in colour, illuminated the vast arid landscape with a strange light. The sun had a transparent gauzy veil so that the eyes could be easily fixed upon it. The grey mother-of-pearl tone turned into a sheet of silver which broke up as the clouds were torn apart and the silver sun, enveloped in the same gauzy grey light, was seen to whirl and turn in the circle of broken clouds. A cry went up from every mouth, and people fell on their knees on the muddy ground. The light turned a beautiful blue as if it had come through the stained-glass windows of a cathedral and spread itself over the people who knelt with out-stretched hands. The blue faded slowly and then the light seemed to pass through yellow glass. Yellow stains fell against white handkerchiefs, against the dark skirts of the women. They were repeated on the trees, on the stones and on the *serra*. People wept and prayed with uncovered heads in the presence of a miracle they had awaited. The seconds seemed like hours, so vivid were they.

One Avelino de Almeida recorded this account for *O Seculo*:

From the road, where the vehicles were parked and where hundreds of people who had not dared to brave the mud were congregated, one could see the immense multitude turn towards the sun, which appeared free from clouds and in its zenith. It looked like a plaque of dull silver and it was possible to look at it without the least discomfort. It might have been an eclipse which was taking place. But at that moment a great shout went up and one could hear the spectators nearest at hand shouting, 'A miracle! A miracle!'

Before the astonished eyes of the crowd, whose aspect was biblical as they stood bareheaded, eagerly searching the sky, the sun trembled, made sudden incredible movements outside all cosmic laws – the sun 'danced' according to the typical expression of the people . . . People then began to ask each other what they had seen. The great majority admitted to having seen the trembling and the dancing of the sun; others affirmed that they saw the face of the Blessed Virgin; others, again, swore that the sun whirled on itself like a giant catherine wheel, and that it lowered itself to the earth as if to burn it in its rays. Some said they saw it change colours successively . . .

Dr Almeida Garrett, described as a 'well-known professor of Coimbra', wrote to an interested colleague of the event:

It must have been nearly two o'clock by the legal time, and about midday by the sun. The sun, a few moments before, had broken through the thick layer of clouds which hid it and shone clearly and intensely. I veered to the magnet which seemed to be drawing all eyes and saw it as a disc with a clean-cut rim, luminous and shining, but which did not hurt the eyes. I do not agree with the comparison which I have heard made in Fatima – that of a dull silver disc. It was a clearer, richer brighter colour, having something of the lustre of a pearl. It did not in the least resemble the moon on a clear night because one saw it and felt it to be a living body. It was not spheric like the moon nor did it have the same colour, tone, or shading. It looked like a glazed wheel made of mother of pearl. It could not be confused, either, with the sun seen through fog (for there was no fog at the time), because it was not opaque, diffused, or veiled. In Fatima it gave light and heat and appeared clear-cut with a well-defined rim.

The sky was mottled with light cirrus clouds with the blue coming through here and there but sometimes the sun stood out in patches of clear sky. The clouds passed from west to east and did not obscure the light of the sun, giving the impression of passing behind it, though sometimes these flecks of white took on tones of pink or diaphanous blue as they passed before the sun.

It was a remarkable fact that one could fix one's eyes on this brazier of heat and light without any pain in the eyes or blinding of the retina. The phenomenon, except for two interruptions when the sun seemed to send out rays of refulgent heat which obliged us to look away, must have lasted about ten minutes.

The sun's disc did not remain immobile. This was not the sparkling of a heavenly body for it spun round on itself in a mad whirl. Then, suddenly, one heard a clamour, a cry of anguish breaking from all the people. The sun, whirling wildly, seemed to loosen itself from the firmament and advance threateningly upon the earth as if to crush us with its hugh and fiery weight. The sensation during those moments was terrible.

During the solar phenomenon, which I have just described in detail, there were changes of colour in the atmosphere. Looking at the sun, I noticed that everything around was becoming darkened. I looked first at the nearest objects and then extended my glance further afield as far as the horizon. I saw everything an amethyst colour. Objects around me, the sky and the atmosphere, were of the same colour. An oak tree nearby threw a shadow of this colour on the ground.

Fearing that I was suffering from an affection of the retina, an improbable explanation because in that case one could not see things purple coloured, I turned away and shut my eyes, keeping my hands before them to intercept the light. With my back still turned, I opened my eyes and saw that the landscape was the same purple colour as before.

The impression was not that of an eclipse, and while looking at the sun I noticed that the atmosphere had cleared. Soon after I heard a peasant who was near me shout, 'Look, that lady is all yellow!'

And in fact everything, both near and far, had changed, taking on the colour of old yellow damask. People looked as if they were suffering from jaundice and I recall a sensation of amusement at seeing them look so ugly and unattractive. My own hand was the same colour. All the phenomena which I have described were observed by me in a calm and serene state of mind and without any emotional disturbance. It is for others to interpret and explain them.

The above account is about the most thorough that seems to be available, and various abbreviated versions of it have been quoted in a number of places. The three brief pieces that round off our reports of the solar miracle have seldom appeared since 1917. The first was written by a Dr Domingos Pinto Coelho for the newspaper *Ordem*:

The sun, at one moment surrounded with scarlet flame, at another aureoled in yellow and deep purple, seemed to be in an exceedingly fast and whirling movement, at times appearing to be loosened from the sky and to be approaching the earth, strongly radiating heat.

A priest, Manuel Pereira da Silva, wrote a letter to a friend on the night of the event:

The sun appeared with its circumference well-defined. It came down as if to the height of the clouds and began to whirl giddily upon itself like a captive ball of fire. With some interruptions this lasted about eight minutes. The atmosphere darkened and the features of each person became yellow. Everyone knelt even in the mud . . .

Finally, part of a letter written by the illustriously named Dona Maria do Carmo da Cruz Menezes:

Suddenly the rain stopped and the sun broke through, casting its rays upon the earth. It seemed to be falling on that vast crowd of people and it spun like a firewheel, taking on all the colours of the rainbow. We ourselves took on those colours, with our clothes and even the earth itself. One heard cries and saw many people in tears. Deeply impressed, I said to myself, 'My God, how great is your power!'

Assessing the solar miracle

The preceding accounts constitute most of the available evidence for the events of Fatima, which are not easily related to any other single historical event. Unless one is prepared to take up a position based more on belief than on evidence, these events remain confusing and mystifying. Simply, the phenomenon is unique, and though the 'silver disc' passage makes it sound like a number of UFO cases, little of the other material really fits into that context. Much has been made of the 'falling leaf' motion, apparently favoured by the operators of a number of UFOs as a way of approaching the earth. But it is clear from these accounts that this was an illusion of movement at Fatima, not movement itself. There is not a single UFO case (Close Encounter of the Second Kind, I suppose) that resembles Fatima in more than a few, not necessarily connected, details. Certainly there is none that I can recall in which the percipients changed colour, or in which there was any optical or psychological effect that made it seem that such a change had occurred; the comparison does not seem to be a very helpful one, when there are so many anomalies to unravel.

I shall return to the solar miracle when we discuss the evidence presented by all the visions and apparitions; but there is one brief comment to be made. All the reports that mention the state of the sky seem to imply that the 'sun', or whatever it may have been, appeared through a specific hole in the clouds, and was framed by them. Assuming that there would have been thick cloud over the rest of the sky to cause the heavy rain that persisted until the time the 'solar miracle' began, might it not have been the case that the *real* sun itself was actually obscured throughout the course of the phenomenon? And that if this was so, could the object that was seen have been something else entirely? After all, Garrett does write of the clouds appearing to pass 'behind' the 'sun', and there is no independent evidence to suggest that anything at all odd happened to the sun that day. This is not to say that a miraculous, stupendous, incomprehensible event did not occur; but it may be helpful to leave the 'sun' out of the problem altogether, and to look for an explanation based more firmly on the evidence than on the catchphrases of the contemporary press.

The problem of Lucia's memoirs

There are a number of dubious factors in the Fatima story as it has come down to us since about 1945. Most of them centre around the *Memoirs of Sister Mary Lucia of the Immaculate Heart*. At the age of fourteen, Lucia, the only surviving Fatima visionary, entered a strict convent school and on 24 October 1925, she became a nun. She remained within the walls of various religious houses till her death. The first of the *Memoirs* were written late in 1935 – more than eighteen years after the events – and the last in 1941. All of them seem to have been published together, though initially to a very limited readership, in 1942 – a quarter of a century on.

Spending over twenty years in the quiet and seclusion of a religious house, cut off from the normal run of daily life, undoubtedly reliving the events of 1917 time and again, is not the best background for recalling precise details of what must have been deeply traumatic events in the life of a young and innocent child. It would have taken an incredible memory, and a staggering degree of objectivity, for these memoirs to have been an accurate record of what actually happened.

There is only space here to look at the reports of visions 'additional' to those of May to October 1917. There are a number of them. So far as my research has been able to establish, none were ever made known at the time they occurred, or even before the publication of Lucia's memoirs. Two are of little relevance to our investigation. They are claimed to have taken place on 10 December 1925 (The Virgin and the Child Jesus) and 15 February 1926 (the Child Jesus alone).

Of greater significance, because they are said to have occurred before May 1917, are those of 1915 and 1916. The 1915 report concerned, to put it in Lucia's own words: 'A figure poised in the air above the trees; it looked like a statue made of snow . . . It looked like a person wrapped up in a sheet . . . you couldn't make out any eyes or hands on it.' Another child (there were supposedly three others, unnamed, who witnessed the phenomenon) apparently described it as a headless body dressed in white.

Lucia reports several apparitions in 1916, of an angel, 'fourteen or fifteen years old, whiter than snow, transparent as crystal when the sun shines through it, and of great beauty'. He introduced himself variously as the Angel of Peace and the Guardian Angel of Portugal. He taught the children (Lucia says that Francisco and Jacinta were with her on each occasion – who can tell?) a prayer, and hinted at plans and sacrifices to come. If these accounts are true, they shed a very different light on the supposed spontaneity of the events of 1917. If not, we can perhaps excuse the confusion, or falsehood, whichever it was, in view of Lucia's strange and restricted life.

The Fatima story is probably, by now, an amalgam of fact, hearsay, and wishful thinking. All we know about it with any certainty is what is said to have happened during the solar miracle to those that witnessed it. Of the real nature of the children's encounter with a figure they took to be the Virgin Mary we know remarkably little for certain, and that is a less than satisfactory situation in a case on which so much belief and analysis has been based.

SEVEN:
'It looked as if she had an electric bulb inside'
BEAURAING, BELGIUM, 1932

After the undoubted wonders that were witnessed at Fatima – though who would dare say for certain what was their cause or source – the next series of visions to win wide popular approval may seem like something of a disappointment. It has all the characteristics of the visions we have considered so far: the child witnesses; the rural location; the messages, and so on. Yet within a few months of the visions beginning, even leading Catholic scholars of the Marian tradition, who were prepared to accept Lourdes at face value, were expressing serious doubts about their authenticity.

Consequently, it is a little difficult to find objective accounts of the apparitions reported at Beauraing. Because the Catholic scholars – particularly men such as Hellé and Thurston[10] wrote of it so harshly at an early stage, I have found no non-Catholic account of any worth at all. Similarly, because what might be seen as the 'intellectuals' of the Church were unconvinced, the advocates of Beauraing have been apt to redress the balance by going to the other extreme. The Beauraing visions find their way into most books concerning the visions of the Virgin, but are usually treated rather briefly and rather naively.

Beauraing is a large village about sixty miles south-east of Brussels and a few miles from the French border. It is in

the Walloon – French-speaking – part of Belgium, and
the Virgin is said to have spoken in French during the
visions. There is no evidence to suggest that it was an area
of any marked poverty, though the events occurred
during the years of the Depression; it seems that the
primarily agrarian economy of the area was sound and
that though there was some local political unrest, as there
was on a national scale, the children involved were
unlikely to have been affected by either social upheaval
or personal hardship. In 1932 there were some 2000
people living in Beauraing. Five of them, all children,
claimed to have witnessed the series of visions that led to
a remarkably high level of claimed religious experience in
the area right through to the start of the Second World
War. We shall only consider the first series of visions; few
commentators would argue that those that followed were
any more than the product of mild hysteria and wishful
thinking.

The witnesses came from just two families, both established in Beauraing for at least two generations. They
were Fernande Voisin, born 21 June 1917; her sister
Gilberte, born 20 June 1919; and her brother Albert,
born 3 November 1921; Andrée Degeimbre, born 19
April 1918, and Gilberte Degeimbre, born 13 August
1923. The two families were friends, but the children
were not related. M. Voisin worked on the railway, and
had a reputation as a half-hearted socialist; his wife ran a
small hardware shop. Their children had been to catechism
classes, but there seems to have been little enthusiasm for
religion in the family. The father of Andrée and the
younger Gilberte had died, and their widowed mother ran
the home alone. She was not known as being religiously
active.

Whatever the overt religious attitudes of the parents
may have been, there is no escaping the fact that the first
key vision occurred in a religious context. Gilberte
Voisin attended the local Academy, which was run by the
Sisters of Christian Doctrine. The story that persistently
turns up is that she was sent there because M. Voisin

The witnesses at Beauraing.

thought that the nuns would make her eat her meals; this looks an unlikely explanation. In any event, on the evening of 29 November 1932, Giberte's brother and sister, Albert and Fernande, together with their friends Andrée and Gilberte Degeimbre, went to collect Gilberte from the convent school; to do so they passed near a little grotto set up by the nuns, which represented that at Lourdes. They actually made a detour to visit it.

The children rang the bell at the convent door. While they waited, the story goes, one or more of the children looked back towards the grotto, and a railway viaduct that stood above it. Versions differ (and I find this discouraging) as to who spoke first. Most have Albert saying something like, 'Look, it's the Blessed Virgin dressed in white, walking along the viaduct.' Others, probably more accurately, put two lines of dialogue before this, along the lines of, 'I see a light', said by Albert or Andrée, and one of the others replying, 'It must be the headlight of a car'

Whichever is right, a nun came out into the garden at

the children's insistence, but she could see nothing out of the ordinary, and told them not to be silly. By the time she had gone in, all the children were convinced – or had at least convinced each other – that they had seen the Blessed Virgin, whatever anyone else thought. During the following night, Gilberte Degeimbre is said to have spoken in her sleep, saying, 'Look how lovely she is'.

From the very next day onwards, the children started attending daily at the same time and place as the first vision had occurred; some days they went more than once. This certainly suggests that one or more of the children was well-acquainted with the history of other visions of the Virgin. November 30th brought a repeat of the previous day's incidents, but on 1 December the lady had moved a little and was nearly at ground level by a hawthorn bush near the gate. A halo of golden rays was observed round her head, and for the first time the children fell to their knees in prayer. It seems that the vision came and went on three or four separate occasions that evening, and not always seen by all of the children.

On 2 December the vision spoke for the first time, not surprisingly to Albert. There is some disagreement as to exactly what was said, but Hellé[6] and Don Sharkey,[11] ardent critic and convinced advocate, more or less agree on:

Albert: Are you the Immaculate Virgin?

Vision: [Nodded head.]

Albert: What do you want?

Vision: Be very good.

Albert: I promise that we'll be very good.

And when the children returned again at 9 pm.

Vision: Will you really be very good?

Andrée: Yes, yes. We will.

Albert claimed an exclusive vision the same night: he reported that the vision had smiled at him.

December 3rd produces conflicting reports. The children did not go to the garden, that much is certain. The pro-vision accounts say it was because Mother Theophile, who ran the convent and is often cast as the villainess of the piece, forbade them to do so. Hellé says it was because the Voisin children were too busy attending a political meeting relating to some important elections. However, 150 spectators turned up: news of a vision seems to spread uncontrollably, wherever it occurs.

The next evening, the five children were back as usual, along with assorted spectators and two chronic invalids: a blinded adult, and a child of eight who was paralysed. All knelt, and Albert took the initiative in speaking to the vision he said had appeared. Perhaps bearing Fatima in mind he asked: 'Holy Virgin, we beseech you to cure, please, Monsieur Havenne and little Joseph. Tell us what day we must return here.' The vision replied, 'The day of the Immaculate Conception'. Albert said, 'Thank you Holy Virgin. I asked you for these cures, but you will only make them if you wish to grant us a favour.'

Then Fernande asked her first question, 'Must we have a chapel built here for you?' 'Yes', replied the vision.

One account, by John Beevers,[12] claims that on the same night, though later, Albert alone initiated the healing of a ten-year-old girl, Paulette Dereppe, one of whose legs was covered in suppurating sores.

The pattern should now be clear. The five children, with Albert as their catalyst if not, in deference to age, actually their leader, had already introduced to this series of visions the key elements of previous ones. The kneeling to say the rosary, to encourage the vision to appear, in some sort of magical rite; the declaration that the vision is the Immaculate Conception; the request to build a chapel; the promise of a future date when something dramatic would happen; the daily attendance at the site of the first vision; even the element of the vision appearing in a tree, as it had done at Fatima. It must be stressed that in almost all these respects the leading questions were asked by the children, and the initiatives were taken by them. They seemed to know the rules by which the apparition game was to be played. Or was it not really the children who determined the rules and the events as they unfolded? Is there another, more remarkable, reason why the same factors repeat in visions widely separated by time and distance?

Albert seemed determined to produce a miracle, and he devoted 5 December to asking the vision: 'If you are the Immaculate Virgin, we beg you to perform in front of everyone as many miracles as you can on Tuesday [the 8th]' He received no reply. The next day his schoolmaster questioned him about the appearance of the vision – apparently the first time he had been seriously interrogated. I quote from Hellé:

He declared that the Blessed Virgin wore a white dress; that possibly she had a blue sash, but that he could hardly see anything but a blue glow; she had no rosary, he said, but kept her hands joined and still. To the question, 'What is the colour of her eyes?' the boy answered, 'Blue'. At this his mother, who was present at the interview, gasped. 'But you didn't tell me that!' she exclaimed. The boy went into greater detail: her dress was draped, her feet rested on a cloud of smoke, etc. Her face, he said, was 'luminous'.

'What do you mean "luminous"?'

'It looked as if she had an electric bulb inside.'

On 7 December the vision was again silent in response to requests for miracles, but on the 8th the effects of modern communications combined with the timeless desire for the miraculous were displayed to the full for the first time. Despite the minimal substance of the visions to date, the word about the 8th of December had been widely broadcast. Seven thousand people came to Beauraing by train alone; up to 15,000 visitors in total had gathered by 6.30 pm in the road beside the school and the convent.

So far as miracles were concerned, nothing happened. The two invalids who had been given this date by Albert made audible and moving pleas to the vision they could neither see nor hear, but which the children assured them was present. They received no cure, no respite even. The children reported that the Virgin stayed only for a short while, and did not make a sound. Many of the onlookers left heartily disappointed, and the only point of interest was that several of the doctors among the huge crowd performed some basic tests on the children while they claimed to be seeing the vision. They attempted to establish whether the children would respond normally to tactile, audible, and visual stimuli, including holding lighted matches near them, and shining torches in their eyes. Out of all the children, and the two invalids, only Gilberte Voisin displayed any clear sign of being in an ecstatic or trance state; the others responded quite normally.

Even if we can accept the early reports of visions at Beauraing as being evidence of events that were in some way more than purely natural ones, I suspect, as do other far more scholarly commentators, that after this failure Beauraing and its visionaries were well on the slippery slope away from authenticity. The children maintained their nightly attendance at the garden, and prayed as usual, but no vision was reported on the 9th, 10th, 11th, or 12th of December. On the 13th and 14th a silent vision was claimed; on the same night a witness, a Dr Saint-Viteux, began to suspect fraud of some kind. Fernande, who was increasingly becoming the inspiration for the five, appeared to give a verbal cue for the others to drop to their knees and report the arrival of the Virgin.

Again, the 15th and 16th brought nothing, but still there were 2000 spectators present on the 17th. On this day a visiting priest suggested they ask what the lady wanted, and Andrée did so: 'At the request of the clergy we ask what you want.' To which the reply came, 'A chapel'. However, on this occasion there seemed to be discussion and disagreement between the children while the vision was in progress, and when each was asked separately, the children could not agree what exactly she *had* said about a chapel – whether she had spoken a full sentence or just two words. Fernande and Andrée even contradicted each other as to whether the lady had opened her arms prior to vanishing.

There was no vision on 18 December, and by now the children seemed to be labouring to obtain any result at all. A silent vision was reported on the 19th and 20th after thirty-nine and twenty-nine rather rushed 'Hail Mary's' respectively. On the 21st, in response to the question, 'Who are you?', again came the reply, 'I am the Immaculate Conception'.

On the next three days the area was artificially lit, and the witnesses intentionally separated and observed among the crowd. A remarkable degree of cohesion in their movements and responses was observed (similar to those that are reported at Garabandal), despite these precautions. This raises the question of whether there was some unconventional form of communication operating between the children. Fernande asked a question, 'Why do you come here?', that had been suggested to her alone by one of the doctors. She alone heard the response, 'So that people will come here on pilgrimage.' There was a growing hostility among the doctors attending at Beauraing.

Christmas Day and Boxing Day brought nothing, and on the 27th a private vision was reported at 9.45 pm, after the crowds had left. On the 28th just under 2000 people (displaying a remarkable determination) heard the children say that the Virgin had appeared to tell them, 'It will soon be my last appearance.'

However, one further factor was to emerge, which is open to two interpretations. Hellé reports that on the morning of 29 December a Dr Maistriaux had distributed pamphlets in which there was 'mention of a golden heart'. That evening Fernande Voisin noticed that the Blessed Virgin, opening her arms, displayed a golden heart. On the next day Andrée, Fernande, and both Gilbertes claimed to have seen the same golden heart. Fernande (alone) said the lady had told her, 'Pray, pray often!'

On 31 December Albert, too, concurred with the vision of the golden heart. Three separate visions of the Virgin were claimed, and Gilberte Voisin said that she had been instructed to 'pray continually'. A marked synchronicity of action among the visionaries was noticed again. On New Year's Day a secretive discussion was observed between Monsieur Voisin, the children's father and Albert, and Fernande actually said that the Virgin had spoken to her, but that she had not listened; a strange attitude indeed.

The vision at Beauraing, 29 December 1932.

On 2 January, Fernande reported that the Blessed Virgin had told her 'Tomorrow I shall speak to each of you in private'. January 3rd saw the last of the visions to these particular children, though they were far from the last around the Beauraing district; for further information about these latter visions see *Beauraing and Other Apparitions* by Father Herbert Thurston.[10] In most of the less critical

Catholic accounts of the subject, Beauraing is referred to in terms of 'The Golden Heart', and the vision as 'The Virgin with the Golden Heart'. It would be strange indeed if the resulting devotion, conversions and healings were the result of a little pamphleteering by a Belgian doctor.

The reports of the last day's events do not in any way enhance the likelihood of their being authentic. The one notable element missing from Bauraing that has been present in other visions has been the passing on of a secret. Now this point is covered, too. It is worth quoting Hellé[6] at some length:

The other children mingled with the crowd; Fernande, alone, remained motionless before the grotto as if she still awaited one last sign. At one moment some of the spectators cried, 'A ball of fire!', but it was only a photographer's flash. Suddenly, Fernande fell to the ground as if struck down. 'Yes, yes', she exclaimed, prostrating herself with hands joined and overcome with a terrible fit of sobbing. The attack lasted some minutes. Fernande had a rapt look. On their return home all the children were crying.

Andrée Degeimbre: The Blessed Virgin said, 'I am the Mother of God, the Queen of Heaven. Pray always. Farewell.'

Gilberte Voisin (upset and sobbing): The Blessed Virgin told me a secret and said 'I will convert all sinners. Farewell.'

Gilberte Degeimbre: A secret, and farewell.

Apparently, Gilberte only came with her news of a secret about ninety minutes after the others had told of theirs. Fernande felt that she had been called to become a nun. Albert felt that the look on the lady's face might have meant that she intended to return. It must have been a very strange time for all of them.

To close the account of this strange, sometimes rather sad case, I turn to *The Sun Her Mantle*.[12] Here, after the final vision, one of the weeping children is reported as

saying to a witness, 'The lovely days are over'.
And so they were.

EIGHT:
'Mama, there's a woman in the garden'
BANNEUX, BELGIUM, JANUARY-MARCH 1933

Only twelve days after the last of the visions were reported at Beauraing, another series of experiences began. As they were also in Belgium, they have naturally been very much overshadowed by Beauraing itself, and by the perfectly reasonable criticisms that were made of that case. But even though the area round Beauraing became a centre of claims of visionary and religious experience right up to the outbreak of war in 1939, it should be pointed out that Banneux was some fifty miles away, not far from the German border, and away from the direct influence of the Beauraing events. Somehow, I feel that both the witnesses and the reported events in this case have the ring of simple honesty about them – an opinion shared by Father Herbert Thurston despite his doubts about Beauraing.[10] This case seems to be closer to the 'surprise' events at La Salette and Pontmain than it does to any kind of conscious or unconscious fraud. It is only unfortunate that so little detailed information is available about the events; I cannot even find an immediate, verbatim first-hand account given by the sole witness, Mariette Beco.

The background at Banneux is one with which we are familiar by now. Mariette had been born on 25 March 1921 – oddly enough, on the Feast of the Annunciation. The family – two adults and seven children – lived in a small, four-roomed house that had been built by Mariette's father, Julien. Three rooms were bedrooms, and one a combined living-room and kitchen. Julien, who had previously been a wire-maker, was usually unemployed and seldom left the house; the family certainly lived in relative poverty. Of course, by 1933 in Belgium, the chance of a child from such a home being educated was far better than it had been for the earlier witnesses in other countries: but Mariette had something of a reputation as a truant, and spent most of her time helping her mother with the younger children. Certainly, she was not overtly

Marriette Beco (holding baby): the witness at Banneux.

religious prior to the visions and seems to have had little understanding of the Catholic faith. However, this aspect is so often over-emphasized in order to enhance the spontaneity of a vision that it is best not to depend too much on any such assessment.

On the evening of 15 January 1933, not much was going on in the Beco household. All of the family had settled down to sleep by seven o'clock, with the exception of Mariette, her mother Louise, and her brother Julien aged ten, who had been out since about midday. An old bed sheet was covering the window of the room, and Mariette occasionally lifted it to see if her brother was arriving home. As she did so, in the darkness, over the patch of scrub that passed for a garden, she thought she could discern the luminous figure of what appeared to be a woman. She called out, 'Mama, there's a woman in the garden' and then, surprisingly for a child who is said to have been less than clever, she decided that it must be an effect caused by the oil lamp behind her. She took it into the other downstairs room, presumably disturbing a number of occupants, to see if the effect changed when the light was cast from a different angle. It seems that her mother was of the opinion that her daughter was seeing ghosts, and said so. Mariette said she thought it was the Most Blessed Virgin.

Moving the oil lamp did not move the lady, and when Louise Beco looked out of the window (so say most, though not all accounts that I have seen) she too perceived a white, humanoid shape, though with no detail. She stuck to her explanation, saying it was a ghost or a witch. This is a very important point, and one that distinguishes Banneux from any other of the 'child witness' cases. Also, if Mariette's mother really did see the figure, then we do have a very rare confirmation of such an apparition, but also some doubt is cast upon the identity of the figure as interpreted by Mariette herself.

For Mariette, though, there was no question as to whom she was seeing. I have said that there is no first-hand report of her description of the figure, but what follows seems to be the substance of what she saw. It comes from *A Woman Clothed with the Sun*,[9] in a section contributed by Don Sharkey, the author of a prominent book that deals favourably with Beauraing:[11]

A great oval light enveloped her body; the gown, which was spotless, and dazzlingly white, chastely closed at the collar and falling in the simple dignity of broad pleats; the sash, an unforgettable sky blue [which Mariette only saw again on a summer day two years later, it is said] loosely fashioned around the waist and terminating in two streamers at the vision's left knee. Covering the lady's head, shoulders and arms was a veil as completely white as her gown, but of a transparent material. The lady was inclined to the left and forward, with the hem of her dress slightly lifted, exposing her right foot crowned with a golden rose. On her right arm hung a rosary of diamond-like brilliancy, whose golden chain and cross was reflected in the light.

An uniquely personal event ended the vision: as Mariette prayed the rosary, she watched the lady do the same. Then she raised her right hand and beckoned toward Mariette with her index finger. Perhaps her mother really did fear ghosts and witches, for her response to the girl's request to go outside was to lock the door; by the time Mariette returned to the window, the vision had gone. Her brother Julien returned soon after, but had seen nothing. Strangely, her father was told nothing of the events until the next day, when he dismissed them as nonsense, though his wife and child apparently concurred independently as to where in the garden the vision had stood.

The vision seems to have had an immediate effect on Mariette's behaviour. On the next day, Monday, she attended school for the first time in several weeks. She confided her story to a close friend who, with Mariette's permission, went to see the village priest, Father Jamin. He was less than impressed by what he was told, deciding that it was all a product of the proximity of Beauraing in both time and distance.

On the Tuesday, Mariette displayed an unusual interest in learning the catechism. It is clear that her faith had undergone a revival, to say the least, and she began praying regularly. Nor was there to be just the one vision. The second one occurred on the Wednesday night, the 18th, and it contains elements reminiscent of a number of other cases, before and since. Just before 7 pm, despite the bitter cold, she went out into the garden and knelt on the frozen ground to say her rosary. Her description of the arrival of the Virgin reads like many religious experiences before, and a number of UFO cases since. The Virgin seems actually to have flown to the spot, at first appearing minute but apparently increasing in size as she swooped down between the crests of two pine trees. She halted some five feet from where the girl knelt: 'her feet did not touch the ground, but rested on a greyish cloud some fifteen inches above the frozen earth'. Her appearance was the same as before, except that she now wore a stylized halo, made of rays of light cut neatly into a disc shape.

After a time, while her father went off on his bicycle to seek the priest, Mariette stood and, when challenged as to what she was doing, said that the vision was beckoning her to follow. Still praying, she walked some 150 yards up the road, dropping suddenly to her knees three times on the way. Eventually she reached what the more romanticized accounts refer to as a 'previously unknown spring' and what the more prosaic call a 'small stream by the road'. The lady spoke for the first time, saying, 'Place your hands in the water'. Mariette did so, and the lady said, 'This stream is reserved for me', and then, 'Au revoir'.

Mariette was also heard by witnesses to repeat these two phrases and the vision ended much as it had begun, with the lady receding into the air above the pines near the ditch.

The next day both Father Jamin and a Benedictine priest visited the Beco household. Strangely, though, it seems that he visited neither the house nor the spring or stream again, merely informing his Bishop what he was told by other witnesses. The same night there were eleven other witnesses present, including the local doctor, when Mariette came out of the house and knelt in the snow. When the lady appeared she asked, as the Benedictine had requested, 'Who are you, Madame?' To which the reply came, 'I am the Virgin of the Poor'. The child was heard to say, 'O, the Virgin of the Poor.' Mariette again went to the stream, where the lady said, 'This spring is reserved for all nations. To relieve the sick.' Then 'I will pray for you. Au revoir.'

Of course, the witnesses only heard Mariette's running account of what was said; the vision and its message were completely unique to Mariette.

The child spent the next day in bed, and her parents only allowed her to go to the garden when she threatened to jump out of the window. This time another doctor and two journalists were present. Mariette asked, 'What do you wish, my beautiful lady?', to which came the response 'I would like a small chapel.' The witnesses just heard the child say, 'O, a small chapel', before she fell unconscious to the ground. Signs of hysteria were beginning to become apparent.

For three weeks Mariette went into the little garden, but reported no vision. Public interest dissipated, and no witnesses came. Mariette had by now started to attend school regularly, and suffered the abuse of other school-children, even to the extent of being bruised round the face.

February 11th was the Feast of Our Lady of Lourdes. A priest and five nuns were visiting the house, and Mariette made a considerable display of religious devotion in the garden. After the eighth decade of the rosary the vision came again and led her to the stream. Later, though not immediately, Mariette reported that the Virgin had said to her: 'I come to relieve suffering' and then 'Au revoir' again, before disappearing. The following Sunday, this now devout child took her first communion.

Another element with which we are familiar arose on Wednesday, 15 February. Three outsiders were present while Mariette communicated. She later reported that the lady had said, 'Believe in me. I will believe in you' (a strange statement if you do really accept that this was the Virgin Mary). She then revealed a secret followed by the admonition that: 'It is for you alone, Mariette. You must not tell it to anyone, not even to your father and mother. Pray a lot.' She left with her usual 'Au revoir'. This is one secret of which I have not even heard a rumour of revelation.

Eight observers were present at the seventh vision, which occurred on 20 February. It seemed to take great effort for Mariette to establish contact with the vision – ten decades of the rosary and a dozen 'Hail Mary's'. It was snowing and the child was obviously uncomfortable and emotional: she cried a lot. The Virgin of the Poor said, 'My dear child, pray a lot', and 'Au revoir', and then left. It seems that the relationship between the child and the vision had become a highly personal one, and Mariette's preoccupation with religion became even more marked.

The eighth and last apparition at Banneux, on 2 March 1933, has a distinct tinge of sadness to it. Five adult witnesses watched Mariette pray vehemently, reach out her arms in welcome, pray again, then say, 'Yes, yes', as she flung herself to the ground, 'where she lay huddled, hiccuping out "Hail Mary's" as she sobbed convulsively. The rain resumed its downpour.

Later, she told the witnesses that the Virgin had only said, 'I am the mother of the Saviour, Mother of God. Pray a lot. Adieu.' The adieu was not an 'au revoir', and it was final.

There is little more to be said about Banneux. As with almost all the major visions its authenticity was largely agreed by its local Bishop, and it is now the site of a magnificent array of buildings such as would grace any other centre of pilgrimage and healing. The evidence, actually, is far from overwhelming, but almost all commentators seem to agree that there was something 'right' about Banneux and Mariette Beco, that was perhaps 'wrong' with Beauraing.

NINE:
'Before, the cup was filling up. Now it is flowing over.'
GARABANDAL, SPAIN, 1961- 1965

If evidence and authenticity were to be related to effective publicity and the vehemence of the advocates of a case, then Garabandal would be much the most famous of all Marian apparitions. All over the world there are centres devoted to 'Our Lady of Mount Carmel', occupied in distributing literature about the visions that is as literate as it is well-produced. There are a number of of first-rate books by responsible Catholic commentators that put the case for the visions and the visionaries in clear and intelligent terms. There is a film made by American devotees, and a BBC *Everyman* video and film also being shown widely. It is a modern vision, and it has been afforded all the advantages of modern techniques of communication. There is even a regular magazine.

Yet, somehow, among conventional Catholics in Britain at any rate, the Garabandal visions mean surprisingly little. And even in Spain itself, in the Diocese of Santander, the visions have not been permitted the sort of approval of the Church authorities that was so easily given to most of the other events that we have considered. The result seems to be that Garabandal has to some extent – while not seeming to stray far from standard Catholic doctrine in most of its content – become a cult by itself, in which the Virgin Mary is the central figure and the visionaries her prophets, set apart from the rest of humanity by reason of their experience. The place itself has also achieved a kind of sanctity, because there is an expectation of a warning to come, of a miracle to be performed there, and of a permanent sign that will be visible to all who visit the pines at Garabandal, where it will be set. This sort of situation does not even prevail at Lourdes or Fatima, and it is in this context that we should consider what is reported to have happened at Garabandal.

There were four children involved at Garabandal, almost always experiencing the same visions at the same time, but clearly led by one child in particular. The names of the witnesses were Conchita Gonzalez, Loli (properly Maria Dolores) Mazon, Jacinta Gonzalez (all these three aged twelve at the time of the first vision) and Mari Cruz Gonzalez, aged eleven. Though three shared the same surname, they were not directly related, and each had her own home. All were of peasant stock, but none appear to have been subject to any poverty or hardship. They were well known to each other, attending the same small school, though they were not always on the best of terms. Socially, and in the course of the visions, Conchita seems to have paired off with Mari Cruz, and Loli with Jacinta.

The number of reported visions – a total of about 2000, often occurring more than once in a day – makes it impossible to record them individually, and it appears that no one has done so. It is undoubtedly the early reports on which we should concentrate, where there is likely to have been a greater degree of spontaneity. In the great majority of the reports there is little to distinguish one from another, and it will suffice to give a few examples.

For those who like to see a plan behind the choice of visionaries – such as those who devalue La Salette because of the adult life of the visionaries – Garabandal is not encouraging. On Sunday 18 June 1961, after morning mass had been said by a visiting priest (Garabandal not having one of its own) and after many of the devout villagers had returned to the church in the afternoon to say the rosary together, Conchita and Mary Cruz sneaked off to scrump apples from the schoolmaster's garden. Loli and Jacinta caught them at it, threatened to tell on them, but then relented and joined in the escapade. By 8.30 pm they had a good stock of apples, and set off. It seems that they began to feel guilty, because, according to one early account, they decided that their good or guardian angel needed appeasing; and so, in the words of Conchita's diary (unfortunately only commenced in the following year, 1962):

We began to gather stones and threw them with all our strength to the left side, where the devil is said to be . . . When we got tired of throwing stones, and were more satisfied with ourselves, we began to play marbles with little stones on the ground. Suddenly, a very beautiful figure appeared to me, shining brilliantly, without hurting my eyes. The other girls, Jacinta, Loli, and Mary Cruz on seeing me in that state thought that I was having an attack, since I was saying with my hands joined together, 'Oh . . . Oh . . . Oh!' As they were going to call my mother, they found themselves in the same state I was. And they exclaimed together: 'Oh, an angel!' Then there was a short silence among the four of us, and he suddenly disappeared.

This brief account gives some clues to the nature of these visions. It is easy to see (from the game with the stones to the appearance of the angel) how close are the parallels with the events at Fatima, a story that the four girls probably knew very well. There was clearly an interest in angels, a belief in them; they felt there might be an angel around before ever one appeared. Most important, the vision 'happened' to Conchita a few moments before it 'happened' to the others, a feature that is frequently repeated. It is not difficult to see a dominant personality, and a possible degree of telepathy or some other form of psychic contact at work here.

The description of the angel given by Conchita is intriguing:

He was wearing a long, seamless blue robe. He had fairly big

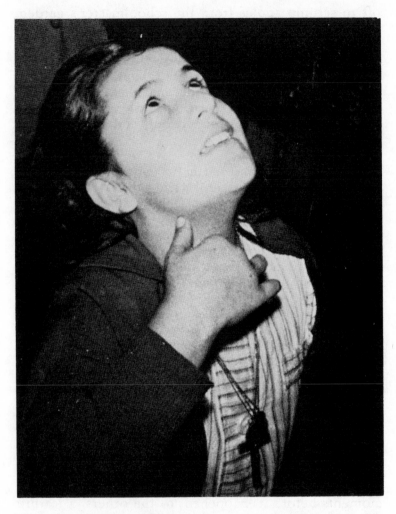

Maria Dolores in ecstasy at Garabandal.

pink wings. His face was small; it wasn't long, and wasn't round either. His eyes were black. He had fine hands and short finger-nails. His feet weren't in sight. He looked about nine years old. But, although he was a child to look at, he gave the impression of being very strong.

This really does seem to be the stuff of archetypes, of aliens, fairies, angels, or whatever other non-human visitor you can think of.

It is not surprising to find that the same time the next day saw the children back at the same spot; this is almost an established pattern with Marian apparitions. The children saw nothing, but that evening the first of what became known as the 'locutions' occurred. There are said to have been several hundred of these. At about 9.45 that evening Conchita was praying in her room when she heard a voice say, 'Do not worry. You will see me again.' It is said that the other three girls heard the same words at the same time.

On the next day, 20 June, Conchita's mother was unwilling to let her go, but eventually the four children made their way to the 'calleja', or sunken lane, on the edge of the village where the first vision had occurred. Nothing happened there so they went to the church. As they rose from their knees there the four of them saw a brilliant flash of light, but nothing else. On the next evening, they had knelt to say the rosary when, for the first time, the four of them went into an ecstatic state, heads thrown back, eyes unblinking, as shown in the photographs. Several observers watched this happen. Later, the girls said that the angel had appeared, but had said nothing.

They gave, it appears, similar reports on six of the next nine days, but on 1 July the angel spoke for the first time, saying that on the next day the Virgin would appear, 'As Our Lady of Mount Carmel'. She duly appeared. Conchita gives an account of it in her diary:

At each side of her there stood an angel. One was St Michael; we did not know the other but he was dressed in the same way; one would have said that they were twins.

Beside the angel on the right, on a level with Our Lady, we saw a very large eye, which seemed to us to be the eye of God.

On that day, we said a lot to Our Lady, and she to us. We told her everything. We told her how we went to the fields, for hay making, that we were sunburnt, and that we had the grass in heaps. She laughed as we were telling her so many things.

For those with some knowledge of the Illuminati stories, another report of this vision is of interest: 'On the Virgin's right, they could see a square of red framing a triangle with an eye and some writing. The lettering was in an odd oriental script.'

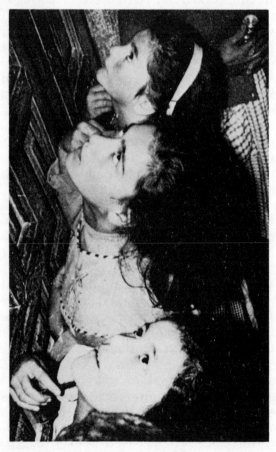

Jacinta, Conchita and Maria Dolores in ecstasy at the closed church door in Garabandal.

Conchita's report of this first meeting with the Virgin seems to typify most of the others. There was much discussion. A great deal of small talk concerning the everyday lives of the girls. It was undoubtedly the most direct and lasting relationship of any that we shall see, and it may well be partly because of this that the more conservative areas of the Church find it so hard to accept the Garabandal vision as genuine. However, there were also dire warnings to the world, and the customary mixture of threats and promises.

Firstly, however, as this is a thread we are following through all the visions, the fullest description that I can find, which is Conchita's, of the Virgin herself:

Our Lady comes wearing a white robe and blue cloak. She has a crown of golden stars: her feet are not visible. Her hands are slender with a scapular on her right wrist. The scapular is reddish. Her hair is long, wavy, and dark brown, parted in the middle. Her face is long, her nose is long and slender and her mouth is dainty and very lovely: her lips are just a little bit thick. Her complexion is quite dark but lighter than the angel's and it is a very beautiful voice, very unusual. I cannot explain it. There is no woman who is like Our Lady, either in voice or in any way at all. Our Lady seems to be about eighteen years old.

There is no doubting the genuineness of the ecstatic states in which the four girls found themselves, or of the extraordinary degree of communication between them, even when separated from each other by the crowd. Or of the remarkable nature of the 'ecstatic marches', sometimes backwards, arm in arm, down steep and stony trackways without ever missing a step. These are strange phenomena indeed, and well worth the closest study. But they are the sort of phenomena encountered and reported in other situations, far removed from this kind of religious experience. What could be said to provide actual evidence of the genuineness of the visions at Garabandal? What could separate them from the other modern visions that have virtually been ignored apart from a brief flurry of initial publicity?

Two particular claims are made at Garabandal. One is of a physical miracle, supposedly predicted before the event. The children, from early in the series of visions, had been receiving the Eucharist from the Virgin, though it was not visible to observers. On 18 July 1961 (most of the dramatic events occurred early in the sequence) it is claimed that, just round the corner from her own house, Conchita fell to her knees in ecstasy, put out her tongue, and on it appeared a luminous white Host, the communion wafer. It is perhaps a little surprising that such an apparently spontaneous event should have been so well attended, but a short film was taken of it (see illustration), and other coherent witnesses were there, one of whom commented, 'It did not seem to have been deposited there but might be described rather as having materialized there, faster than the human eye could see.' It is not, of course possible to say what exactly happened on this occasion, or how such an event could take place. But it remains a remarkable feature of a rather confusing series of visions.

The second claim for Garabandal derives from the messages of warning given by the Virgin, and supposedly commanded by her to be published widely. The messages frame the 2000 visions and hundreds of locutions, one near the beginning, and one near the end of the events, nearly four years later. The first 'Formal Message', as they are known to distinguish them from the conversations with the children, was given on 4 July 1961, and made public on 18 October the same year. It runs as follows:

We must make many sacrifices, perform much penance and visit the Blessed Sacrament regularly. But first, we must lead good lives. If we do not, a chastisement will befall us. The cup is already filling up and if we do not change, a very great chastisement will come upon us.

The second Formal Message was received on 18 June 1965. It may possibly include a comment on the refusal of the Church authorities to accept the visions:

As my message of 18 October has not been complied with and has not been made known to the world, I am advising you that this is the last one. Before, the cup was filling up. Now it is flowing over. Many cardinals, many bishops, and many priests are on the road to perdition, and are taking many souls with them. Less and less importance is being given to the Eucharist. You should turn the wrath of God away from yourselves by your efforts. If you ask his forgiveness with sincere hearts, He will pardon you. I, your mother, through the intercession of St Michael the Archangel, ask you to amend your lives. You are

The 'Miracle of the Host' at Garabandal.

now receiving the last warnings. I love you very much and do not want your condemnation. Pray to Us with sincerity and we will grant your requests. You should make more sacrifices. Think about the passion of Jesus.

The final element of Garabandal is related to these warnings. It is a prophecy, of no evidential value yet because it has not come to pass; Conchita is said to know the date of its commencement. Apparently, there is to be a divine warning which will be visible all over the world. This will be followed (at eight-thirty in the evening of a Thursday which is also the feast-day of a saint who is a martyr of the Eucharist) by a miracle at Garabandal itself, of which a permanent reminder will be left there among the pines. If the sign and the miracle are not heeded, then dreadful tribulation – presumably the end of the world as we know it – will follow. There is much here that is reminiscent of the Fatima prophecies. And as with Fatima we will have to suspend judgement, on this aspect, for a while at least.

TEN:
MODERN VISIONS

It may not be easy to understand why some of the cases we have looked at in this book have achieved the fame and followers they undoubtedly have: Beauraing and Garabandal, in particular, spring to mind. There seems to be no good reason why *all* these cases should have achieved such importance, though most of them deserve their place in the present survey. There have been hundreds of other visions of the Virgin Mary, even since 1830 and reports continue to come in, mainly from Europe, at the rate of at least two or three a year. Recently, most cases have found it difficult to obtain ecclesiastical approval of any kind, and consequently their fame has largely depended on the whims of the media and on the efforts of the little groups of believers who will always spread the news of such visions to the best of their ability. Perhaps if some of these recent visions had occurred a century ago they might now be famous, their visionaries held in the highest respect, and the customary tales of prophecy and healing duly recorded, in the subjective style that has done earlier events such a disservice. If a vision were to occur now, it might be possible to assess its veracity; but if no such vision occurs in the next decade or so, we shall have reason to doubt whether any ever has.

What follows is, so to speak, the Apocrypha to the Old and New Testaments of the previous visions. A strange mixture of cases – some clearly less than convincing, others that could easily have replaced some of the visions we have dealt with in the previous chapters. These cases are the more interesting because they take us to some surprising places for Marian apparitions – such as Wales, Hungary, Yugoslavia, Egypt, and the USA. Some of the accounts come from rather odd places – such as the *Michael Fighting Quarterly* – and from private, ultra-conservative Catholic sources, whose members could be seen as having something to prove. But they are still an important part of our evidence, even if proof and verification of their occurrence is hard to come by.

Robinsonville

The first of these cases takes us, for the first time, to North America – to Robinsonville, Wisconsin, to be precise. Here, in the autumn of 1859 Adele Briss, the teenage daughter of a Belgian immigrant family, twice saw a lady in white while walking along an Indian trail. She was a devout girl, already thinking of a future as a missionary, and when she told her confessor of what she had seen he sent someone to accompany her to the scene of the vision, where the figure appeared again, though only to Adele. The lady is described as being clothed in dazzling white with a yellow sash, a crown of stars round her head and long, wavy, golden hair. Adele asked her who she was, and said she replied, 'I am the Queen of Heaven, who prays for the conversion of sinners, and I wish you to do the same.' The figure then spoke a few more sentences about how Adele should teach religion to others, and promised her help. She then disappeared, rising slowly into the air surrounded by a cloud of incense, and Adele fainted. In the following years her father built a small log chapel on the spot, and Adele became Sister Adele and organized the building of a convent and school which she ran. Later, she met with diocesan disapproval, was refused the sacraments, and threatened with excommunication if she persisted in telling the story of her visions.

Pellevoisin

The case of Pellevoisin is unusual in that it involves a possibly 'miraculous' cure that happened to the visionary herself. In other cases, such as that of Bernadette of Lourdes, healing seems to have been utterly denied to the originator of the shrine. The woman concerned, Estelle Faguette, had been born in 1843, and put to school with the Sisters of Charity in Paris, where she would certainly have been made well aware of the Miraculous Medal and of La Salette. She entered a religious order but had to leave after contracting tuberculosis. She was found employment with the Duchess of Rochefoucauld, who, when Estelle's health deteriorated further, sent her to be cared for at her château near Pellevoisin. There, Estelle displayed her devotion to the Virgin Mary by leaving a letter, pleading for healing and a chance to be well enough to support herself, at a Lourdes grotto in the grounds.

On 14 February 1876, Estelle was in bed when, she reported, she saw the devil appear. Almost immediately the Virgin, all in white, appeared. She said, 'Fear nothing, you know very well that you are my daughter. Courage! Be patient. My son consents to be moved. You will suffer another five days in honour of the Five Wounds of my Son. On Saturday you will either be dead or cured. If my Son gives you back your life, I want you to spread my glory.'

For the next three nights the devil appeared first, then the Virgin, who always spoke, though saying little of import. On the fifth night the devil did not appear, and instead Estelle saw a stone tablet on which was inscribed the words, 'I invoked Mary in the depth of my misery. From her Son she obtained my complete cure. Estelle F.'

After listening to what her visitor had to say, a great spasm of pain shook Estelle and she felt that she was cured. Certainly, her physical condition seemed to confirm this. She had no more visions till July, then three more in September, one in November, and one in December. Most of the messages she received concerned devotion to the Sacred Heart of Mary, and much of Estelle's life from thereon was committed to making and distributing scapulars bearing its image.

Initially, Pellevoisin received considerable Church approval, but this ended in the early years of the present century. Though the scapular and some of the Virgin's words to Estelle were accepted as being of genuine worth and significance, no authenticity has ever been attributed to the visions themselves, or the 'miracle' of her healing, although Pellevoisin had the potential of a Pontmain or a Banneux.

Llanthony

The supposed apparitions at Llanthony, Wales, in August and September 1880 are unique in at least one respect; they occurred (if they occurred at all) in what was meant to be a religious establishment of the Church of England, even if a somewhat fringe one. The Abbey at Llanthony had been founded by Father Ignatius, a British aristocrat whose devotion to the Virgin Mary was the driving force of his life. He had surrounded himself wih a few individuals, both adults and children, who seemed to be of a like mind, and there is no doubt that there was a constant atmosphere of expectation that wondrous things might happen; but it is worth quoting briefly from the Abbey Chronicle for 1880:

30.8.1880 (9.30 am)
Sister Janet saw the Sacrament begin to manifest itself outside the massive doors of the Tabernacle. Very shadowy at first, it gradually became perfectly distinct, and remained so for some time... In the evening of this Monday, August 30th, four of the boys were playing in the Abbot's Meadow between Vespers and Compline – it was just eight o'clock and still light – although getting dusk. John Stewart, a boy of twelve-and-a-half years, was waiting for his turn to run in the game, when he suddenly saw a bright dazzling figure gliding across the meadow towards him; a halo of glory shone out from the figure all around in an oval form. The form was of a woman, a veil hung over the head

and face, the hands were both raised as if in blessing. It approached very slowly . . . They saw the beautiful form enter the hedge, and after remaining there in the light for a few moments, passed through the bush and vanished . . . The appearance was like the pictures of the 'Immaculate Conception'.

4.9.1880
[Written by Brother Dunstan, who has just seen the rhubarb bush mentioned in the last excerpt aglow with bright light]
   I suggested that, if it really was the Blessed Virgin, if we sung the 'Ave Maria' she might appear again. So we began to sing the 'Ave' and on our doing so, we at once perceived the form of a woman surrounded by light at the top of the meadow by the gate. Slowly the form and the light advanced towards the already illuminated bush.

This apparition, though it remained vague, was said to have lasted two hours. Though the grass around was 'wringing wet with a heavy dew', it was said (much as at Knock in the previous year) that the ground around the bush remained dry and warm.

There was supposed to have been a brief vision the following day, but the most dramatic event (at least to judge by the description) was still to come – somewhat orchestrated by the good Father Ignatius:

15.9.1880
The Reverend Father then said, 'Now, sing an 'Ave' in honour of the Blessed Virgin herself.' We had no sooner begun it than the whole heavens and mountains broke forth in bulging circles of light, circles pushing out from circles – the light poured upon our faces and the buildings where we stood and in the central circle stood a most Majestic Heavenly Form, robed in flowing drapery. The Form was gigantic, but seemed to be reduced to human size as it approached. The Figure stood sideways, facing the Holy Bush. The Vision was most distinct and the details were very clear; but it was in the 'twinkling of an eye' . . . A few minutes after this Mr E. from Oxford and one of the boys, saw the shadowy form of the Blessed Virgin in light,

by the enclosure gate with uplifted hands. This is the last of the visions vouchsafed by God's mercy to us.

Tilly-sur-Seulles

Leaving aside the dubious cases of Neuholz, in Alsace, where in 1871 three young children saw a white figure they identified as the Virgin brandishing a sword against the Prussians; Marpingen, in the Rheinland, where in 1876 three children saw a 'white lady' and 20,000 people arrived within a week claiming a large number of cures; and Mettenbuch, in Bavaria, where in 1877 three little girls claimed visions, not only of the Virgin and the Infant Jesus, but of many other Biblical characters too, we move on to another odd and confusing case. (The three cases mentioned briefly above can be found in Father Herbert Thurston's excellent survey of the Marian apparitions.[10]

The events at Tilly-sur-Seulles, in Calvados, France, began in March 1896, when an aerial vision of the Virgin was seen on several successive days by the teaching nuns of the school there, and by some fifty to sixty of the pupils; the figure seemed to appear 'above a field hard by, close to a big elm'. The testimony of the nuns and the children as to what they saw seems genuine, though obviously the repetition of the same vision is not as evidential as a succession of different visions would be. What lends a certain quaintness to the case is the visions reported at the same place by other 'visionaries', often strangers drawn by the news of the apparition of the Virgin. A number of these reported conventional 'religious' visions, while others saw devils and hell and all kinds of strange effects. Often, such visions were thought to have been inspired by the devil, unlike the original vision, which was regarded as coming from heaven. Unusually, most of the later 'voyantes' seem to have been adults and to have often fallen into states of ecstasy verging on hysteria, sometimes simultaneously, each claiming different visions! One of the younger visionaries, Jeanne Bellanger, aged thirteen, had trances in which her body was all contorted, and while she knelt, her whole spine curved back until her neck touched the heels of her boots. The sight was so painful that it made many of those who looked on positively ill.' Unfortunately, no thorough and objective study of the events at Tilly seems to have been attempted, and it is now far too late to try to undertake one. I suspect that the first event and the consequent repetitions might have achieved a far greater respectability if it had not been for the others. The situation is only further confused by the fact that the occultist Vintras, who had lived at Tilly over half a century previously, had apparently predicted that it would be the scene of visions.

The aftermath of Beauraing

I mentioned previously that Beauraing, and Banneux to a lesser extent, were followed by a succession of visions and visionaries right up to the outbreak of the Second World War. It may well be that this sort of 'enthusiasm' led to something of a devaluation of the significance of such visions, for none has been taken so seriously since. Initially, the interest centred round some of those who had been 'cured' at Beauraing, and there are dependable reports of over 150,000 people gathering at the town some time after the original visions had finished.

The first major vision after Banneux was in September, 1933, when one Leonie Van Dyck of Onkerzele, East Flanders, claimed a succession of apparitions in which, unusually, the Virgin appeared in different guises. This lady seems to have predicted forthcoming war and disaster for Belgium (not a bad guess, if true), initiated the discovery of a spring, and called for a chapel to be built. Many thousands of people came to prayer meetings at Onkerzele.

Another Flemish apparition was reported at Etikhove in October of the same year, when a local painter and glazier, Omer Eeneman, 'saw a ball of fire which parted to reveal a human figure'. The vision later appeared complete with scroll at her feet and, as at Onkerzele, participated in the events. Other typical visions of these troubled years in Belgium occurred at Houlteau Chaineux and (a series) at Melen, near Liège. It can safely be said that as time went on, the reports became less convincing, and the claims of visions patently less authentic.

Montichiari

This is a peculiar case, taken from one of the more extreme sources that I have had access to. The sole witness is a Pierina Gilli, born in 1911. In 1947 she was working as a nurse at the hospital in Montichiari, Italy, when the Virgin, crying, appeared to her dressed in purple with a white veil: 'Her breast was pierced by three large swords.' Her only words were: 'Prayer, Sacrifice, Penitence!' Pierina had a further vision a short time later, when the figure gave detailed instructions concerning 'a more efficacious Marian devotion within institutes and religious congregations'. Most of her concern seemed to be with looseness of doctrine and behaviour within religious orders. A further vision was reported on 13 January 1951, speaking in much the same terms: Pierina also reported hearing a chorus of angels singing psalms.

Ohio

The *Michael Fighting* newspaper, published quarterly in remarkable numbers, contains a number of accounts of visions of which little else is known. Unfortunately, the emphasis is more on the messages received than on the witnesses and the circumstances of the visions. For instance, visions at Kerizinen, Brittany, in October 1955 are mentioned, but there are just no facts to recount. One case that is covered in rather greater detail concerns the appearances of 'Our Lady of America' to a nun in the order of the Sisters of the Precious Blood in Ohio, USA. There is reason to believe this was in the Cincinnati area. This nun seems to have had 'locutions' or messages from a number of religious figures over a period of years, and the Virgin Mary first appeared to her on 25 September 1956. She was still doing so in 1980. The description of her is very familiar, but there is considerable stress laid on

her heart, 'encircled with red roses, the symbol of suffering
as it was revealed to me, and sending forth flames of fire'.
Her messages are very much of the post-war kind, full of
warnings of persecution, suffering, and disaster, if men
and the Church do not change their ways.

Mariamakk
I cannot vouch for the authenticity of the following story.
It is quoted from the *Michael Journal*, but comes originally
from the *Recueil Marial* of one Brother Albert. In the
original it is entitled 'It is She who brought me back from
Siberia!'

For many years now Janos lingers in a camp deep in Siberia.
Without the memory of his dear Ilona Helen, he would have
despaired a long time ago. Thanks to her, he keeps a ray of
hope; he begins to recite the prayers of his youth. This gives
him courage. His faith in God, his confidence in the 'Great
Lady of the Magyars' are rewarded by an ever growing faith and
an invincible hope.

On a summer night of 1958, Janos feels a push against his
arm, and a voice tells him 'Get up, put on your clothes'. 'What
are you saying?' The voice repeats: 'Get up, put on your
clothes. Put on your soldier boots.'

Janos complies. No one wakes up in the barrack.

'Come,' the voice says, and he feels himself pulled by the
arm. The door grated as it opened, a sentinel stands there
within ten steps, a machine gun on his shoulder. He sees
nothing, he hears nothing . . . Janos and his mysterious guide
run towards the camp's gate. Searchlights light up the camp.
Janos is surrounded with light, and instinctively he stops. But his
guide tells him in a calm voice: 'Come, do not be afraid.' It is
then that, for the first time, Janos sees in the beam of the
searchlights the guide who is leading him out of the camps: it is
a great lady wearing a dark blue coat, with a face of beautiful
and singular whiteness. Suddenly the lights go out and the two
sentinels who guard the entrance to the camp see nothing. The
Lady opens the large door with great ease. Janos thinks he will
die from fear.

'Come quickly,' says the Lady. She closes the door without rushing like one would do in the daytime. They quickly cross the public square to get to the closest station. Twice they come across a patrol that observes nothing abnormal. Once at the station the Lady says, 'In two minutes time a freight train will come into the station, and in its middle there will be a passenger car. Get on it, you will need no ticket, no identification card.' The Lady then hands him a bundle saying: 'This will be useful during the journey.' Then she added: 'In Budapest everything will go well also.' The train comes. While Janos is looking in her direction, the Lady disappears, to Janos' great regret. He would have so much liked to thank Her and to say 'Goodbye'.

The train stops. Janos gets on. A few travellers: they are sleeping. A controller comes along; he stops before Janos but says nothing. Janos wonders whether he is dreaming, everything seems mysterious. Each time a controller comes into the car Janos thinks he will die of fear, but each time the controller just seems to ignore him.

Slowly, Janos starts to settle down. He opens the bundle that he received from the Lady, and finds it contains bread, cheese and meat. There is water on the car. The travel lasts four days and four nights, but they finally reach the Hungarian border, where he must change trains. There are no problems, not on the train, nor in the station, nor on the streets of Budapest. No one seems to pay any attention to him. It is strange, since his convict clothes and his big iron shoes should draw the people's attention.

Night is coming when Janos arrives before his house; would Ilona, his wife, still be there? He rings the bell. A strange woman answers. 'Does Mrs Ilona Balogh still live here?' 'Yes, but in the attic. She will be back in half an hour.' Seeing the peculiar attire of the stranger, she brings herself to ask, 'Would you have some news concerning Mr Janos Balogh? Did you know that he disappeared more than twelve years ago? His wife, Ilona, continues to hope that he will return some day. Almost every day she goes to Mariamakk to pray for his return. She certainly went there again today.'

Janos does not answer and he does not make himself known; he remains outside on the street. A half hour later Ilona comes back, and he recognizes her at once. 'Ilona,' he cries out. 'Janos, oh Janos! I knew you would return.'

The next day they return to Mariamakk to thank the Virgin, Help of Prisoners. Janos has never been there before, and when he sees the Madonna's statue he cries out, 'But it is She. Yes, I recognize Her. It is She who brought me back from Siberia . . .

Zeitoun

In complete contrast to the previous case – which admittedly strains credibility, but adds a touch of individual compassion that often seems to be missing in these encounters – come the mass apparitions of Zeitoun, a suburb of Cairo, in Egypt. Many commentators have regarded these apparitions as being very important, but so far as *evidence* is concerned I think it is of very limited value; in some ways, the illustration of one of the figures seen there sums the whole issue up. However, a number of points need to be made about Zeitoun.

The visions there lasted from 2 April 1968 till well into 1971. In the first year they were quite frequent, but tailed off during 1969 to about one a month during 1970. It seems likely that well over a million people witnessed what took place. Yet there are less than a hundred witness reports openly in circulation, the photos are generally poor in quality, and uncertain in detail, and there is no movie film that I have been able to find. There is a handful of books on the subject, but none of them really come to grips with the supposed extent of the visions. Surely, if they were all that has been claimed, they would have achieved far greater fame? They would have been a milestone in both psychological and religious experience; this they clearly are not.

Though these were repeated, public phenomena, occurring in a civilized country, I will freely admit that I do not understand what happened at Zeitoun, any more than I understand why there are no films, why the media showed so little interest, or why so few people know anything about such an apparently major event. The apparitions took place on the roof of the Coptic Church,

A Zeitoun apparition.

known as St Mary's of Zeitoun, an imposing domed building. It stood opposite a public transport garage, which was eventually demolished to make room for more people to see the events – for a small charge. The first report, by some of the workers at the garage, is typical of many later ones. They saw a figure of a female in white, 'kneeling beside the cross on top of the dome'. It was thought that the woman was about to commit suicide by jumping, and someone went off to call the fire brigade. Then the figure moved to a standing position, and almost at once someone cried out, 'The Virgin Mary!' Soon after, what appeared to be a flight of luminous birds – possibly doves – flew around the head of the figure, and the whole scene just faded away into the darkness.

Some reports speak of witnesses seeing the visions 'in flashes only' – it would seem not to have been a wholly objective experience, but rather one that depended upon long and regular observation, after which the vision could be intermittently seen. Many people travelled there and waited for several nights, but saw nothing at all; there seems to be no logical or predictable pattern to the appearances. They were investigated by a commission set up by the Coptic Pope Kyrillos VI (not, as has sometimes been assumed, by the Pope in Rome), and its conclusions were that the visions were actually of the Virgin Mary. The Coptic Bishop Samuel reported one of the early visions:

At 2.45 in the morning the Blessed Virgin Mary appeared in a complete luminous body as a radiant phosphorescent statue. After a short while the apparition vanished. It reappeared at four o'clock and remained until five o'clock – dawn. The scene was overwhelming and magnificent. The apparition walked towards the west, sometimes moving its hands in blessing, and sometimes bowing repeatedly. A halo of light surrounded its head. I saw some glittering beings around the apparition. They looked like stars, rather blue in colour . . .

As I have mentioned, there are other accounts, but few if any stray far from this impression of an animated statue – sometimes appearing to be holding a young child – and of bird-like luminous shapes both heralding and accompanying the vision's appearance. A number of persuasive accounts of cures exist, and it is clear that though this apparition did not occur within the usual Catholic context, both Catholics and some popular parapsychologists have been willing to accept them at face value. There are some similarities with the events at Knock in 1879, but overall it does seem to be a rather odd way for the Mother of Christ to behave. Not a word was said by the figure during any of the appearances.

Bayside, New York
The tale of Veronica Leuken, the 'Bayside Seeress', is sad, and verifiably true. A friend of mine went to stay with some of her followers in 1979. She claims to have had visions since 1968, when St Teresa started appearing to her; the first appearance of 'Our Lady', as she is referred

The 'Ball of Redemption' at Bayside, New York.

to, took place on 7 April 1970. After that she appeared at first in the grounds of an old local church, and later in the more convenient 'Vatican Pavilion Site' in Flushing Meadow Park. At these sites Veronica, and Veronica alone, has received countless messages and visions from a variety of Catholic religious figures, but particularly from both Christ and Mary. The distribution of these messages, mostly in a paper entitled *Roses*, issued regularly in large numbers, is a fine example of the use of modern communications. Wherever in the world I have contacted the traditionalist end of the Roman Catholic fraternity copies of *Roses* have been sent to me. The majority of issues are full of warnings against immorality, pornography, liberal Catholicism, Satan, fake popes, dissolute cardinals, and so on, all supposedly quoted from the lengthy messages Veronica receives from Mary, Jesus and others. In truth, though there have been substantial public gatherings at Flushing Meadow, it seems that there have only ever been a small number of active supporters around Veronica

Leuken, and that as she has been seriously ill for several years she plays only a minor part in the present organization.

Perhaps the single most intriguing feature of the Bayside events have been polaroid photographs taken with cameras that she has had blessed by her heavenly visitors (see illustration opposite). These supposedly feature a forewarning of the 'Ball of Redemption' that is threatening the world with destruction if we do not change our evil ways. To some people, the 'Ball of Redemption' is reminiscent of someone leaving a thumb or forefinger in front of the camera lens. This is not an explanation readily accepted by believers.

Citluk

It is interesting that, as I write this, two quite notable series of apparitions still appear to be in progress. Cases that demand to be taken seriously are not all that common. The first of these two cases is that of the tiny village of Medjugorje near Citluk, in Yugoslavia. The apparitions have been a cause of some concern to the Communist authorities, and have caused upheaval in the area. The case is a typical one. The first vision was on 24 June 1981, when six children – four girls and two boys – aged between ten and seventeen saw the figure of the Virgin holding the child Jesus, on a hill near the village. One of the boys described her as 'dressed in grey clothes reaching to the ankles. Her shoulders were covered with a white mantle, and her head surrounded by a brilliant crown of stars.' She was said to have 'floated over the meadow'.

It will come as no great surprise to hear that the children immediately made a point of returning to the site of the apparition the next day, or that the figure appeared daily, except on four days, for about five months. Prayer, penance and fasting seem to have been at the heart of her messages, and five secrets were given to the children; these have probably already been transmitted to the Pope. After November access to the original site was restricted by the authorities, and the visions are said to have continued in the children's homes and in the local church. Up to 30,000 people are said to have gathered in the meadow on occasions, and a number of specific cures have been claimed. All the children appear to have been asked by the figure to enter religious orders or become priests, and as at Garabandal some sort of 'visible sign' has been promised 'when least expected'. In reply to the children's questions, the figure has described herself as 'The Queen of Peace'. It is now unclear what the future of the apparitions may be – they seem to have become very closely linked with the cause and the advocates of Croatian nationalism.

La Talaudiere

This recent case is both fascinating in its own right, and doubly so because it has attracted the attention of some French paranormal researchers, who have provided some excellent background information that is sadly lacking in other cases. The only witness is Blandine Piegay, aged fourteen, the youngest of five children of an unemployed miner who is nearly blind as a result of an accident. The family seems to be devoutly Catholic, and Blandine has been reliably described as 'emotionally fragile'.

Initially, there seems to have been a series of poltergeist-like physical disturbances in the house, all involving Blandine. Then, in October 1981, she reported that she had been visited by an otherwise unknown Saint, Nicole, who had died at the age of fourteen and is now an angel. Nicole said that Blandine would start menstruating three weeks later, and that the disturbances would then cease. She also said that Blandine would then be visited by 'the mother of the Saviour'.

On 31 October 1981, the Virgin appeared to Blandine in the kitchen at home. She told the child to ask her parents to leave the room, and said she would see her the next Saturday. At this, or another early vision, a total of 90 visions in all was spoken of. The visions continued each Saturday, at home, at about 5 pm, and numerous messages were given. Most of these concerned the sort of conservatism to which we have become accustomed by now, together with the usual warnings: 'If the world continues to offend God, I will not be able to stay the arm of my son. There will be punishments. There will be wars.' The traditional items were also requested: the saying of the rosary, the building of a chapel or basilica, to be named Notre Dame de Talaudiere.

During May 1982, the frequency of the visions increased, and the vision began appearing on odd-numbered days. On the 34th appearance she said she would appear in the family garden – now widely termed a cabbage patch, as in the media phrase 'The Virgin and the Cabbage Patch' – on the afternoon of Easter Day. A letter from Blandine's mother describing the events in the house was duplicated and distributed, and as a result there were between 3000 and 5000 people at the house on the Easter Sunday afternoon. Unfortunately, the crowd was disappointed, at least to begin with. Blandine's father addressed them, and said that because it was curiosity, not devotion, that had led most of the crowd to be there, all future visions would occur inside the house. The next development is best told by a British researcher, Hilary Evans:

The crowd were not all disappointed; many stared at the sun – despite warnings from left-wing mayor Pierre Damon, who went among the crowd with a loudhailer warning people not to stare at the sun. However, those who did were rewarded, seeing a cross on the sun's face, seeing it rotate, and change colour from mauve to red to green. During the following days some thirty had to receive medical treatment for eye afflictions.

Both the parish priest and the Bishop of St Etienne have taken a sceptical attitude to these claims, probably with some reason, and have permitted them no official approval. Pilgrims still arrive, if only in small numbers, and there is really no telling what is going on inside the house now. Sadly, we end up with as little detailed information about the actual visions in a current case as we have about ones that occurred over a century ago. This appears to be an inevitable problem when dealing with this subject – I look forward to a case where it will be possible for investigators of standing to become involved in the documentation of a series of visions. This is the right time for such a study – all we require is the place and the opportunity.

ELEVEN:
ASSESSING THE EVIDENCE

This book *is* about evidence – not speculation. But having presented the main facts concerning the eight most important visionary events of the past two centuries, there is a clear need to try to make some sense of the evidence; to present some possible explanations; to see if any one explanation can apply to such a variety of events. It must also be stressed that numerically, at least, these cases represent only the tip of the iceberg. If we consider the period 1830-1982, then it seems likely that the number of different *sites* of Marian apparitions is well in excess of 200, all round the world. Further, these are only the visions that have become known to the media, and to authors like myself: there must be countless others that have gone unreported, for one reason or another. Within that 200, there are undoubtedly many weak cases, and some that have never been afforded any credibility – for example, the 'pseudo-visionaries' at Lourdes. Up to twenty other people, mostly young girls, claimed to have had visions similar to those of Bernardette Soubirous. They were never taken seriously – it is just the sort of hysteria that affects young girls – yet they still appear in the lists of visions and visionaries. In addition there are many more obscure reports; and if one takes into account the number of visions apparently experienced at, say, Garabandal or Zeitoun, the scale of the phenomena becomes clear.

Faced with such a quantity of evidence, it would be foolhardy to say that all of those who reported visions were deliberately lying; that each and every visionary set out to fabricate evidence, to deceive believers and investigators alike. About a quarter of the cases are French, about another quarter are Italian. If we look specifically at the traditions of visions in those two countries, there is simply no evidence to suggest that the visionaries displayed any sign of being liars, or that the visions attracted the sort of people who lied habitually. In a handful of cases, there is evidence of profits being made – the prices charged for accommodation around Knock is an example – but even then this seldom benefited the witnesses.

If we accept that, whatever else the witnesses may have been, they were not liars, then there must be some explanation for what those witnesses believed were genuine experiences. There are two broad options: either the visions were of the Virgin Mary, or they were not. This brings us back to the questions I raised in the introduction: what does the evidence, once established, actually prove? That the witnesses had visions that they believed to be of the Virgin Mary? Or that the witnesses had visions *of* the Virgin Mary?

The more important, more significant option is clearly the second. It is the option accepted, if not exactly supported officially, by the Roman Catholic Church, and believed in by millions. If it should prove to be true, and verifiable, then it would imply something momentous about the purpose and meaning of life on earth. It is an option that implies a direct, physical link, a route, between earth and heaven, between God and man. Catholic theology certainly permits such a physical transfer, in one direction at least. To quote Leo Trese in *The Faith Explained*: 'In the fourth mystery of the Rosary, and annually on the feast of the Assumption, we celebrate the fact that Mary's body, after death, was reunited with her soul in Heaven.'

To put it in simple, non-theological terms, not only is such a journey possible, but should the Mother of Christ *wish* to make a physical return from heaven she, uniquely, has a physical form in which to appear. And if it is accepted that the journey can take place in one direction, then why not the other?

A theological possibility is one thing; that an event should actually have occurred is quite another. If even one real, physical appearance of the Virgin Mary did take place before even one of the witnesses, is there any process or method, comprehensible to science, by which it could have happened? Could we go one step beyond simply *believing* in the event and suggest a plausible explanation for *how* the event came about? I do not think we can. If the experiences were genuine, if genuine physical appearances of the Virgin Mary have taken place, then it is by means that are wholly beyond our comprehension. We would be dealing not just with divine intervention, but with direct divine action. Perhaps this is why, when the local bishops responsible for pronouncing on the veracity of visions make their declarations, they do so in such vague terms. Writing of Fatima the Bishop of Leiria (a position created more or less for the purpose) was barely enthusiastic:

We have pleasure, first to declare as worthy of credence the visions of the shepherds at the Cova da Iria in the parish of Fatima, of this diocese, on the 13th day of the month from May to October 1917.

And second, to permit officially the devotions to Our Lady of Fatima.

The Bishop of Liège, concerning Banneux, is keener but little more specific:

We believe in all conscience that we can and ought to admit without reserve this fact; namely the truth of the eight apparitions of the Blessed Virgin to Mariette Beco on the 15th, 18th, 19th, and 20th of January, the 11th, 15th, and 20th of February, and the 2nd of March 1933.

The traditional religious and theological approach is of little help to us in trying to assess the significance and meaning of the evidence. It is one way – a very natural way – of approaching phenomena that are well beyond our usual frame of reference, but faith and belief must be recognized as such. At this stage, I think we must return to a straightforward analysis of the evidence, on the assumption that we are looking for a force and an intelligence that is more than human. To establish an identity, a police detective will look for relationships, similarities and individual characteristics. Can a similar process lead to a clear conclusion with the evidence we have here?

The evidence of the witnesses

1. *Arrival*
There is no consistency in the manner of the arrival or appearance of the visions. In most of the 'private' cases it has been sudden – often indoors. But in the major, popularly accepted cases it has generally been outdoors. In most of the cases there has been an element of 'light' or luminescence in the initial appearance; preceding the daylight cases: making the nocturnal appearances visible. Also, there are frequent light effects close to or decorating the figure. Motion is often reported during the commencement of the vision. No two cases are identical, but there is this in common between the cases – a distinct impression that there is a considerable usage and output of energy. However, it is not possible to find any marked similarity between a significant proportion of cases.

2. *Departure*
This is often a strange business, lacking in grace or apparent logic. At La Salette the lady disappeared from the head downwards, leaving only a brightness. At Lourdes, it was a sudden vanishing. At Pontmain the disappearance was the other way up – we have Eugene's lovely remark about her going into a kind of bag. Of the manner of the

end of the Knock apparition there seems to be no record, though this would have been a vitally important factor. At Fatima, we seem to have a sudden disappearance from the children's point of view, though perhaps not from the point of view of other witnesses. At Beauraing, the figure seems to have come and gone suddenly and frequently. At Banneux, the first vision seems to have been present before Mariette noticed it, and on other occasions the figure glided in from the sky. The records of the Virgin's leaving are not as thorough as they might be, however, and I do not think that much can be made of this varied evidence.

3. *What the vision looked like*

In the majority of cases we have a clear and thorough description of the physical appearance of the vision, often dwelling more on clothing than on the description of the person. There is no doubt that history and tradition have done much to shape the idea that we now have of many of the visions – particularly at Lourdes, where both age and stature seem to have become substantially distorted. There is some overall similarity in the style of dress, and of the face – a young woman of Anglo-Saxon appearance and complexion, with blue and white clothing, including a veil, and often a crown or halo of some kind; but it is clear that over the centuries there have been considerable variations. There is little similarity between the young Mexican girl at Guadalupe, the teenager first seen at Lourdes, and the witty, relatively sophisticated visitor at Garabandal. And even if we come to more minor differences, of dress and decoration, no two visions seem to come clad the same. If we are talking about a physical visitor to the visionaries, then must we also think in terms of some heavenly wardrobe, full of the matching outfits worn by the visions over the years?

Such variations will not matter much to the believer – they may even enhance the wonder inherent in the event. But there are few of us who deal with reports of visionary experience, in paranormal or religious contexts, who would not now readily admit that there is a strong subjective element in what is experienced. To put it simply – the experience may be genuine, as may any communication that takes place during it. Yet the vision, the way in which the witness perceives the source of the phenomenon or the communication, may be a construct of the witness's mind; a way of making sense of what is happening to them, because we human beings are not accustomed to talking to people who are not palpably there! Such a thought process might account for the extreme beauty of the figures reported by the witnesses, though the nature of the beauty might differ from one witness to another. What believer would not instinctively attribute the rarest of beauty to the Virgin Mary? Yet how many of us have precisely the same idea of beauty as anyone else? Nonetheless, if we are to play detective, rather than believer, it has to be said that the evidence points firmly away from the descriptions all referring to the same physical individual.

4. *The content of the communications – and the silent visions*
There are only two notable silent visions, those at Knock and Zeitoun; both are somewhat mysterious. It is not that I expect any vision to behave logically, or in a manner that is reasonable to a modern western mind. But silence communicates nothing when it is combined, in the one case, with total immobility and, in the other, with walking around on the roof of a church, bowing occasionally. It may be that those who see significance in such silence are right. But these silent visions have led only to confusion, and a marked distrust on the part of many commentators.

The majority of visions of the Virgin involve communication, as do visions of other kinds in other parts of the world. This is usually direct speech, but on more than one occasion it has been after the fashion of Pontmain, with 'written' words appearing against some sort of constructed background.

The content of the communications is potentially the most important of the evidence, though much of it hardly seems significant. On the one hand we have the sort of light conversation frequently reported by the witnesses at Garabandal, and at many of the minor visions. On the other we have the elements that can hardly be described as demonstrations of humility; the requests for processions, chapels, basilicas, and so on. These elements may well be an example of witnesses wielding a new-found power over the authorities, who had often troubled them previously. None of this material is evidential.

5. *Prophecies and warnings*

The important parts of the communications divide into two linked subjects. Firstly, prophecies; secondly, warnings. The early prophecies are intriguing, and not a little convincing. There is no doubt that the content of the La Salette messages was made known publicly before those prophecies were fulfilled. Of course, many human beings over the years have proved their ability to prophesy, in various different ways; perhaps the children at La Salette had this ability. If so, did they choose, albeit unconsciously, to communicate this foreknowledge in a way that they knew their friends and parents would understand? The possibilities are many – the apparent truth of the prophecy remains unchanged. The case for later prophecies, not yet fulfilled, is not so clear cut. I have explained my doubts about the time sequence of the revelations said to have been communicated at Fatima, and the Third Prophecy – apparently known but concealed by the Papacy since 1960 – remains a prophecy alone. The same is true of prophecies made at Garabandal, Bayside and the more recent visions. None of them provide evidence for the presence of the Queen of Heaven.

La Salette aside, where the warnings were far more specific and comprehensible than many that followed, much the same criticisms apply to the warnings of doom and disaster. This type of communication, often more of a threat than a warning, is becoming more common. The warnings present a strange contrast to Evangelical and Charismatic expectations of the end of the world. While the Fundamentalists wait for the fulfilment of prophecy, Antichrist, the Tribulation, Armageddon and the rest with an anticipation verging upon glee, the Marian apparitions warn that such an end will only come about if mankind does not change its ways, when Russia is converted, and so on. These kinds of admonishment seem typical of the carrot-and-stick type of religion that has kept adherents within cult groups since the beginning of recorded history. There is, in conclusion, little evidence to be found in any of the communications – not if we are looking for understanding or knowledge that witnesses could only have derived from a supernatural source.

6. *Healings and conversions*

Much of the evidence popularly accepted as supporting the veracity of the visions themselves actually derives from the healings and conversions that followed them. The distinction has to be clearly made. While there have been a great many reports of healing that could well be interpreted in purely conventional ways – and these include early 'officially accepted' cures at both Lourdes and Knock – there are other cases where it is obvious that there is a direct circumstantial link between the shrine where the vision took place and the healing. Such cases can be quoted in relation to almost all of the visions analysed in this book, and in many more besides. Details of such healings may be found in the books listed in the Bibliography.

But fascinating as these healings are, and though they are worthy of attention in their own right, they do not constitute convincing evidence with regard to the content, source, or meaning of the visions themselves. There is no specific case in which the Virgin Mary herself performed an act of healing, and sometimes requests for healing seem to have been virtually snubbed, or at best avoided. Most of the time, the vision seems to have been preoccupied with other matters, and generally the communications only touch on healing when the subject is brought up by the witness. The expectation and belief that healing is a direct consequence of contact of any kind with a vision, or with the place in which a vision has occurred, seem to have been born of the sort of traditions noted earlier in Chapter 1. The modern visions appear to have different preoccupations.

The key point concerning the healings is a straight-forward one. Not all of the visions we have considered seem to be either true or credible; others are even less so. Yet healings are reported in the context of the most dubious and unlikely visions. The visions, indeed, seem to have little to do with the healings. We should not confuse the cause with the effect, and assume that a healing confers some validity upon the event that preceded it. I would suggest that no such link between visions and healings can be proved, even in the case of Lourdes. Consequently, the healings are unlikely to provide us with any useful evidence.

Similar considerations apply to the conversions that often succeed Marian apparitions. At the best of times conversion is a hazardous and tenuous process, dependent more on emotion and circumstance than on an objective consideration of the facts. The sudden sense of being over-whelmed by a hitherto uncomprehended truth – that is how I experienced conversion, anyway – is a powerful, internal shock, possibly deriving from the individual. Frequently, it does not last, and when it does it requires reinforcement; how many of those converted by Billy Graham in the mass rallies of the sixties still follow his brand of Christianity? In the context of the visions of the Virgin, the crowds, the sense of expectancy and the excitement, it is not surprising that amongst those who came as observers many should depart as converts: it is a common part of human experience, only made the more likely by reports of healing and other miracles. But here again, the incidence of conversions seems to have little bearing on the exact nature of the visionary figure. Conversions happen in other circumstances, other faiths. Sometimes the con-version experience is initiated by utter charlatans, plausible though they may be. Conversions are not only the province of the divine.

Taken overall, the evidence of the visions is inconsistent. It does not suggest one clear, physical source for a significant proportion of the events, and is on occasion contradictory. Were I the detective that I mentioned earlier, I should conclude that the visionaries were reporting experiences involving a number of girls and women, of different races, ages and backgrounds, most of them native to the country where the visions appeared. That is, if I accepted their physical reality at all. There are other factors that weigh heavily.

When we move away from what is suggested by theology, or belief, or even the accounts of the visionaries, we are also obliged to consider the reports and claims concerning the visions in the light of common sense. Is there any reason why, if the Virgin Mary chose to return from Heaven, she should appear only to Christians? Why should she be seen mostly by poorly educated young children, living in rural and backward areas? Why should she choose witnesses who barely understand what is happening to them; and why should she communicate so ineffectively that Bernadette Soubirous, for instance, initially believed that she was either a demon or a ghost? Why did she often fail to identify herself clearly, or even remain silent? Why make vague, undated prophecies and give mysterious, though frightening, warnings? Why leave no physical traces, fail to heal when requested repeatedly to do so, yet request chapels and processions? Why did she choose the sites that she did, and the times that she did? Why appear once at La Salette, and thousands of times at Garabandal? In particular, why should she make her identity and her intentions so utterly unclear that thousands of researchers and investigators, and hundreds of books and pamphlets, have consistently failed to make sense of what she has supposedly chosen to do? If such an intelligence should choose to take such a drastic and remarkable course of action, surely her purpose would have been made unequivocally clear?

Yet if we continue to accept that the visionaries were not liars, except perhaps in a handful of instances, we must also accept that they had some sort of genuine experience. Even if this did not involve physical visitations of the Virgin Mary, there must be an explanation for the huge quantity of reported visions that we have considered. This is not the sort of explanation that features in religious history or, perhaps, in the understanding of conventional science. More probably it belongs in another, less well-established, field of study.

The paranormal connection

Though this book is part of a series concerned with the evidence for a wide variety of paranormal or psychic phenomena, I do not want to over-emphasize this aspect. To say that the Virgin Mary is a paranormal event would not only be disrespectful to those whose belief in her is important in their lives: it would also be untrue. We are discussing an aspect of human experience, via the accounts of those who had the experiences: we are not attempting to make this aspect more mysterious or other-worldly than it is. Nonetheless, it is to some areas of paranormal events that it is easiest to relate many of the visions; and there is some statistical evidence to suggest such a correlation, particularly with UFO sightings.

If the visions were not of the Virgin Mary herself, what else could they have been? There is no doubt that the majority are inter-related: witnesses are aware of what has happened to other witnesses previously. The image of the Miraculous Medal recurs; so too does the behaviour of Bernadette at Lourdes. As time has passed it has become easier to detect the different elements that go to make up each visionary experience and its aftermath. Citluk is almost an ideal case: every element is there. Thus, it is not difficult to believe that the recurrence of the visions may be due to some element in the subconscious, a race memory of visions and meetings with the ideal female figure; a memory reinforced each time a visionary's report is made public. Some would have it that belief, like prayer, can *cause* events, could *cause* the visions. This is an idea met in eastern mysticism and magic – a thought-form taking on a will and a substance of its own.

Is there a simpler explanation, or at any rate a more traditionally western one? I have seen it suggested in extreme Protestant religious material that the visions are in fact demonically inspired, that they derive from the devil, that they have been sent to mislead simple human beings from believing in Christ alone and make them worship His mother instead, thus breaking the First Commandment. I have seen it suggested that some or all of the visions are in fact incorrect interpretations of meetings with non-human entities, either from another planet, or time, or dimension. Neither of these two explanations resolve the problem; and there seems to be no evidence to support either view. Similarly, possible links with poltergeist phenomena – which often arise in houses where girls of around the age of puberty live – have been suggested. But though the experiences may be of a similar type and age, which may have some significance, there is no apparent connection between these types of phenomena.

More useful, perhaps, are the correlations with certain types of UFO experience, particularly in view of the frequency with which meetings with aliens are reported by UFO witnesses. Gilbert Cornu, a French UFO researcher, has recorded the numbers of meteorological anomalies that were interpreted as 'divine' manifestations between 1900 and 1980. He found that the numbers increased dramatically from 1947 onwards, the very year that 'flying saucers' became the delight of the media all over the world. Similarly, both he and Italian researchers found that the numbers of reported instances of Marian apparitions rose sharply in 1947, and again during the 1954 wave of UFO sightings in France. The reasons for these correlations is not clear; but they are clearly significant, even if they only indicate that the prevalence of one kind of anomalous event may lead to an upsurge in the occurrence of another.

Regarding the question of entity encounters, the situation is equally unclear. There *ought* to be close links between the visions – in which people, often, though not always, meet a non-human figure from a 'higher' or 'better' place – and UFO close encounters, in which something very similar happens. Yet almost all the elements of the reported experiences are different from each other. While the UFO entities, particularly in so-called 'abduction' cases, may remove witnesses from cars, even from their homes, examine them medically, show them the interiors of spacecraft, give them information about other worlds, and so on, nothing of this nature occurs in any of the Marian visions. The evidence only very rarely involves physical contact; there is no technological context; no infringement of free will; no wish on the part of the vision even to talk about the nature and existence of heaven. The total difference in appearance between the two types of non-human entities could be reasonably explained in terms of expectation and belief; the total difference in approach and behaviour just cannot be set aside. A similar set of objections holds good for suggestions that the visions have some similarity to 'apparition' or 'ghost' cases; the often sophisticated and sequential nature of the visions is virtually unheard of in traditional psychical research.

One group of writers has made a sterling, if rather selective, attempt to analyse the visions, both in the context of the whole range of religious phenomena and in the broader context of the paranormal. Most of them were writing between 1968 and 1980, though one of them, D. Scott Rogo, has gone on to write an excellent account of religious phenomena, *Miracles*,[13] published in 1982.

The writers concerned are John A. Keel,[14] Jaques Vallée,[15] Jerome Clark,[16] and the aforementioned D. Scott Rogo.[17] All were writing, essentially, about the UFO phenomenon, and are widely regarded as being amongst the most prominent thinkers in this field of study. While some of them would perhaps now modify some of their earlier statements, what they were attempting was both original and praiseworthy. They saw a consistent repetition of particular aspects of events and experiences regarded as anomalous and inexplicable, throughout recorded history from pre-biblical times. They acknowledged that these events changed and developed in specifics, but remained much the same in broad context and in the cues – often balls or masses of light – that either heralded or initiated the events. They postulated an original recurring phenomenon that was interpreted differently according to the experience, expectation and possibly the mental and psychological state of the witness. Not surprisingly these writers found the light phenomenon at Fatima, witnessed by onlookers, to be of interest; and the Solar Miracle was positively enthralling. Unfortunately, they seem to have missed the remarkable degree of understanding and synchronicity, observed by witnesses, between the children, even when the latter were split up among the crowds at Fatima, Beauraing, Garabandal, and elsewhere.

In many ways, however, this is not an unreasonable theory. If humans keep on meeting non-humans over a period of thousands of years, are we to conclude that all the witnesses were deluded, or that there exists a huge variety of non-humans waiting to be met? Or would it be more reasonable to suppose that the non-humans come from the same source, and merely *seem* to be different to observers over the years? In my investigations I work on the principle that the most likely explanation is that which is least unlikely. In this instance, the last of the three seems to be the best.

Within this theory the visions of the Virgin (Lourdes, Fatima and Garabandal are those most commonly mentioned) are seen as a stage in the development of the theory as a whole, somewhere between the legends of the 'little people' and the advent of the UFO. In its most basic form the argument is that what looked like the Virgin Mary to a young peasant girl in Catholic Lourdes in 1858 might well look like an extra-terrestrial to a bright, space-age youngster in 1983, though it might actually be neither of those things. If you can accept the principle that people see what they expect to see, or – more obscurely – that witnesses can psychically interact with a vision, shaping it so that others can witness the same phenomenon, then such a theory may well have some validity. It could be seen to apply at Pontmain, Beauraing, Fatima, Garabandal, and even at Zeitoun or La Salette. It is a theory worthy of consideration despite possible objections, including religious ones.

The witness as psychic – a tentative conclusion

There is a subtle difference between presenting the visions as part of a paranormal field theory and suggesting that the factor linking the visionaries may be that they themselves were psychic. It is an idea that has arisen rarely, perhaps because it detracts from the 'holiness' of the events. It is clear that the direct parallels between the visions and paranormal 'events' – UFO sightings, entity encounters, abductions, ghosts, poltergeists, apparitions, lucid dreams, and out-of-body experiences – are few and far between; the visions constitute a phenomenon and a tradition of their own. The parallels that are more plausible are the negative ones, those that detract from the authenticity of the reports. Among these are the lack of convincing photographs, the rural locations of many of the events, the inconsistent reports, the failure of prophecy, and the unsatisfactory witness status in the great majority of cases. Both UFO encounters and Marian apparitions have occurred in great quantity, yet we are unable to agree on even the most basic understanding of them; the evidence for both is so poor that it is almost possible to believe that the confusion is intentional.

The other similarity between the visions and paranormal experiences in general is that the experiences are intensely personal. It is absurd to discuss the visions in terms of group hallucination or mass hysteria. Though massive crowds were often present and desperate to see the vision, to share the experience of the visionaries, there is no convincing instance of this happening: the overall experience of those who came, full of hope, to observe

observe was one of disappointment. Even at Fatima the experiences of the visionaries and the crowd seem to have been mutually exclusive. As with the vast majority of paranormal experiences, all we really know of the visions is what the visionaries have told us.

We seem to have a common sensitivity among the witnesses, a sensitivity that can be interpreted as clairvoyance or psychism – call it what you will. Many of those who achieve fame as psychics in adult life report encounters with figures during their childhood, figures that were invisible to their families and those around them. Had they been raised in a Catholic family, with the knowledge of previous visions reported by other children, might they have reported meeting the Virgin Mary? Is that how it works?

There is more objective evidence of apparently unconventional communication between the witnesses. Studies made of them at Beauraing and Garabandal showed that although separated intentionally in different areas of a crowd, they would respond simultaneously to undetectable stimuli. At Garabandal there were other phenomena; the children seemed to know individually but at the same moment when to attend a vision. They displayed an apparent ability to negotiate treacherous, rocky ground in darkness, going backwards without faltering. There are claims of a public levitation when the four children, arm in arm, crossed a footbridge only wide enough for two of them. The children at La Salette gave out prophecies that proved accurate. The children at Pontmain seemed to know of a vital and unexpected change in the course of an international war. I have suggested that there is no positive *evidence* that the Virgin Mary herself was involved in these experiences. Could the children not, like those who dreamed of screaming children before the disaster at the mining village of Aberfan, have somehow picked up this information themselves? If they did, we must certainly regard them as psychics, if only for those brief minutes or hours. And the control of one of the children over the others – particularly at Fatima – also hints at the exercise of an extraordinarily powerful influence, one that is a very different matter from group hallucination. Could it be that the states of ecstasy sometimes observed during the visions – most frequently at Garabandal – could be either a preparation for the use of psychic faculties, or a symptom of their use? Is the belief and conviction that the Virgin Mary is present a way of overcoming conditioning and inhibition that would normally repress the use of such faculties?

These are questions we cannot yet answer; and unfortunately, unless there is a sequence of cases accessible to competent investigators in the foreseeable future, we may never be able to do so. There seemed to be an opportunity with Blandine Piegay but, as we have seen, discretion was adjudged to be the better part of valour, and the opportunity passed. At present, we have a vast array of evidence that is often inconsistent and contradictory. We cannot say what it *does* prove – only what it does *not*. The evidence we have available does not prove that the visionaries fabricated the accounts of their experiences, nor does it prove that the Virgin Mary, in the physical form she took with her to Heaven, returned to visit one or more individuals at any of the 200 or so sites with which she has been associated during the last 150 years. The truth seems likely to be unrelated to either of these two extreme possibilities. And though it may not actually reveal a major secret about the nature of our existence, there is no doubt that it constitutes one of the most fascinating unanswered questions in the field of anomalous experience. One that warrants, and demands, considerable further investigation.

TWELVE:
A PERSONAL VERDICT

I have been researching the visions of the Virgin for several years, and on the whole I have been disappointed to find that there is less to most of the visions than originally seemed to be the case. In the seven major, speaking visions – La Salette, Lourdes, Pontmain, Fatima, Beauraing, Banneux and Garabandal – we have a total of only nineteen witnesses telling us about the actual visions. All of them are children, most of them barely literate, and having very little experience in life. The contemporary investigation was often shabby and incomplete, and the recording of the witnesses' own accounts often took place far too long after the events for accuracy. There is plenty of evidence, but much of it is of barely acceptable quality; assessing it is fraught with problems.

Consequently, while I am prepared to accept that most of the visions were genuine for the visionaries, I am not convinced that any external force, entity or intelligence had a part in any of the reported visions. The standards of proof required to establish such an event beyond reasonable doubt would of course be very high; but these should not be beyond the capacity of the intelligence supposedly involved to provide. The lack of direction in the visions, if nothing else, leads me to doubt a divine origin.

The best method of approach to such incidents is the one I have already mentioned: to accept as the likeliest explanation for an event the explanation that is least unlikely. Bearing this in mind, I would suggest that what emerges from the stories of the visions may be a contact with some sort of externalized form established by belief and hope over the years, and perceived by those who were prepared for it, who were in the right frame of mind. This frame of mind may be similar to that experienced by Spiritualistic mediums and psychics.

The study of witnesses to Marian apparitions points, for me, towards one conclusion: that these children were more 'aware', more 'sensitive' than others of their age – possibly due to their hard and uncomfortable home life, to their personal beliefs, or to any one or more of a great number of other reasons.

Traditionally, mediums and others have explained their paranormal abilities in terms of 'guides' or other interested parties from the Great Beyond. I was disappointed when Uri Geller, who initially seemed willing to take responsibility for his own talents, chirped up with his tales of helpful extra-terrestrials. Similar stories arose with witches – the healers and mediums of their own day – who would refer their abilities back to some non-human force or other. Aleister Crowley did it – so do certain Christians I have known who, when something they have worked hard at has turned out right, promptly shout 'Praise the Lord'. We may not be very good at taking responsibility for the harm and damage that we do, but we are also very unwilling to take the credit for what could be a little remarkable.

Much of the evidence of the visions rests on hearsay, expectation, and secondhand reports. To go beyond the premise that the child witnesses may be drawing on mental faculties that normally lie dormant we shall need a new source of information. For now, I can only say that I am far from convinced that the Virgin Mary has visited earth during the past 1900 years. But I am more than ever committed to finding out why so many people passionately believe that she has. In the visionaries, we see ordinary people undergoing extraordinary experiences. If we can

find out what uneducated children are able to perceive
that we adults cannot, then our time will not have been
wasted.

BIBLIOGRAPHY AND READING LIST

As previously mentioned, the material drawn on in this book is not the kind to which specific references can easily be given. Much of the book utilizes several sources simultaneously; but wherever possible I have noted below the most useful and objective books on which I have drawn for the narrative accounts of specific cases. Many of these were never published in the UK and are difficult to obtain. There is, however, a wealth of information in the titles listed in the *General* section and many of these contain reliable versions of most of the major cases.

Where a book is specifically referred to in the text it is followed by a number in brackets.

General

Aradi, Zsolt, *The Book of Miracles*, Monarch Publications (USA), 1956.

Beevers, John, *The Sun Her Mantle*, Browne and Nolan, Dublin, 1953 **(12)**.

Delaney, John J. (ed.), *The Woman Clothed with The Sun*, Image Books, New York, 1961 **(9)**.

Gallery, John Ireland, *Mary Versus Lucifer*, Bruce (USA), 1960.

Hellé, Jean, *Miracles*, Burns and Oates, 1953 **(6)**.

Pelletier, Joseph A., *The Immaculate Heart of Mary*, Assumption Publications (USA), 1968.

St John, Bernard, *The Blessed Virgin in the Nineteenth Century*, Burns and Oates, n.d. **(8)**.

Early Visions

Christian Jr., William A., *Apparitions in Late Medieval and Renaissance Spain*, Princeton University Press, 1981 (2).

Fisher, Claude, *Walsingham Lives on*, Catholic Truth Society (London), 1979.

Herolt, Johannes, Miracles of the Blessed Virgin Mary, tr. C.C.S. Bland, Routledge, 1928 (1).

Johnston, Francis, *The Wonder of Guadulupe*, Augustine Publishing Company, Devon, 1981 (3).

Pontmain

Richard, L'Abbé, *The Apparition at Pontmain*, tr. F.C. Husenbeth, Burns and Oates, 1871 (7).

Knock

Rynne, Catherine, *Knock 1879-1979*, Veritas Publications, Dublin, 1979.

Fatima

Barthas, C.C., and Da Fonesca, G., *Our Lady of Fatima*, Clonmore and Reynolds, Dublin, 1947.

de Marchi, John, *Fatima. The Facts*, Mercier Press, Cork, 1950 (18).

Johnston, Francis, Fatima. *The Great Sign*, Augustine Publishing Company, Devon, 1980.

McGlynn, Thomas, *Vision of Fatima*, Skeffington and Son Ltd., 1951.

Pelletier, Joseph A., *Exciting Fatima News*, Assumption Publications (USA), 1975.

Ryan, Finbar, *Our Lady of Fatima*, Richview Press, Dublin, 1939.

Walne, Damien, and Flory, Joan, *Oh, What a Beautiful Lady*, Augustine Publishing Company, Devon, 1980.

La Salette

Carlier, Revd Louis, *The Apparition of Our Lady on the Mountain of La Salette*, Missionaries of La Salette, Connecticut, 1911.

Gouin, Abbé, *Sister Mary of the Cross, Sheperdess of La Salette*, privately published, n.d.

Kennedy, John S., *Light on the Mountain*, Browne and Nolan, Dublin, 1954.

Ullathorne, Most Revd William, *The Holy Mountain of La Salette*, Missionaries of Our Lady of La Salette, 1854 (?) (4).

Lourdes

Andrews, Bernadette, *She Met Our Lady*, Catholic Truth Society (London), 1979.

Deery, Joseph, *Our Lady of Lourdes*, Browne and Nolan, Dublin, 1958.

Estrade, J. B., *The Grotto of Lourdes*, tr. J. H. B. Girdlestone, Art and Book Company, 1912 (?).

Neame, Alan, *The Happening at Lourdes*, Hodder and Stoughton, 1968 (5).

Walne, Damien, and Flory, Joan, *(Oh, Yes . . . I Saw Her*, Dites Publications (UK), 1979.

West, Donald J., *Eleven Lourdes Miracles*, Duckworth, 1957.

Beauraing

Sharkey, Don, and Debergh, Joseph, *Our Lady of Beauraing*, Hanover House (USA), 1958 (11).

Thurston, Herbert, *Beauraing and Other Apparitions*, Burns Oates and Washbourne, 1934 (10).

Banneux

Beevers, John, *Virgin of the Poor*, Abbey Press (USA), 1972.

Garabandal

Laffineur, M., and le Pelletier, M. T., *Star on the Mountain*, Our Lady of Mount Carmel (USA), 1968.

Pelletier, Joseph A., *God Speaks at Garabandal*, Assumption Publications (USA), 1970.

Sanchez-Ventura y Pascual, F., *The Apparitions of Garabandal*, San Miguel Publishing Company, Detroit, 1966.

Modern Visions

Fortean Times, a magazine that usually includes, amongst a vast array of Fortean and anomaly material, full reports of all Marian phenomena as they occur. The address is: BM – Fortean Times, London WC1N 3XX.

Michael Journal (also known as *Michael Fighting*), Rougemont, PQ, Canada.

Assessing the Evidence

Clark, Jerome, and Coleman, Loren, *The Unidentified*, Warner, New York, 1975 (16).

Keel, John A., *UFOs: Operation Trojan Horse*, Putnam, New York, 1970 (14).

Scott Rogo, D., *Miracles. A Parascientific Inquiry into Wondrous Phenomena*, Dial Press, New York, 1982 (13).

    , *The Haunted Universe*, New American Library, New York, 1977 (17).

Vallée, Jacques, *The Invisible College*, E. P. Dutton and Company, 1975 (15).

INDEX